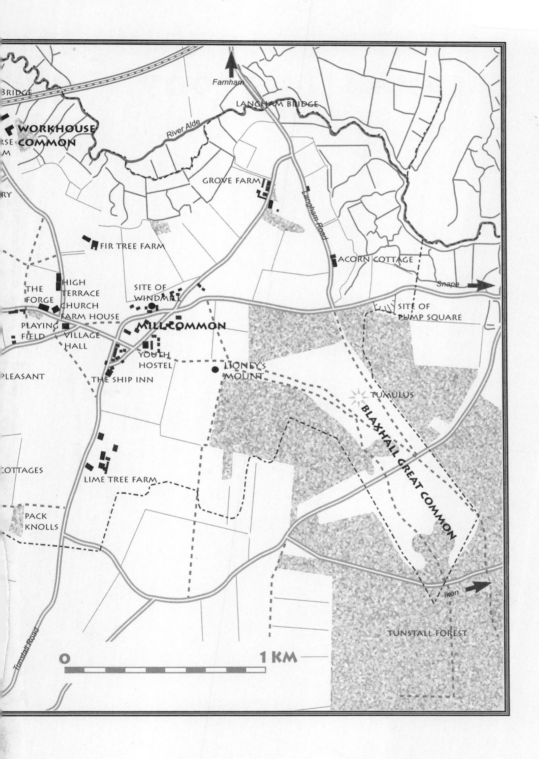

BLAXHALL'S CREATIVE PAST

SNAPSHOTS OF VILLAGE LIFE

Written and researched by the
Blaxhall Archive Group

RODNEY WEST, MAGGIE GRENHAM, DAPHNE GANT, ENA PLANT,

PAUL SMITH, SHANE PICTOR, PETER FLETCHER, RAY POACHER & VIOLET SKEET

THE BLAXHALL ARTIST BY JOHN DAY

THE POET SCULPTOR BY ARTHUR ROPE

HEROES AND UNSUNG HEROES - ORIGINAL RECORDINGS BY GINNY SULLIVAN

DEDICATED TO
NORA AMELIA LING
1921 - 2007
HENRY HAMMOND
1934 - 2008
GEOFF LING
1916 - 2009
REG MANNALL
1926 - 2009

George Smith with his master's sheep, Blaxhall, c.1910

CONTENTS

First published in the United Kingdom in 2009
by the Blaxhall Archive Group, Blaxhall, Suffolk IP12 2DP

British Library Cataloguing in Publication Data
A catalogue record for this book is available from the British
Library

ISBN 978 0 9555389 3 3

Typeset in 11/13 Antigua
Design and layout: Blaxhall Archive Group
Printed by: The Lavenham Press, Lavenham, Suffolk

FOREWORD

This second publication, from the Blaxhall Archive Group, attempts to focus on another facet of the village's social history. The basic rationale is to explore the creative side of just a few of the characters that lived in Blaxhall; the grocer's daughter Ada Mannall and her 20 years of photographing everything of interest; the Blaxhall artist, George Thomas Rope and the Poet Sculptor, Ellen Mary Rope, brother and sister and part of the large, talented, Rope family. Then there are the ordinary men and women who after their day's toil still found time to relax and sing in the pub or parish rooms, act in plays and concerts, play quoits or just, generally be creative.

Like our first book, 'Blaxhall's Living Past', this has been a co-operative enterprise, with members of the archive group researching much of chapter one and transcribing chapter four. But we have also been fortunate to have the assistance of two expert authors, John Day who has studied the work of George Thomas Rope for over forty years and knows everything there is to know about our Blaxhall artist. And then Arthur Rope, who has researched the careers of some of his artistic relations including Ellen Mary Rope culminating in his chapter, the Poet Sculptor, which we hope will be seen as the definitive biography of his great aunt.

Finally, to be allowed to use the valuable resource that is Ginny Sullivan's recordings of her fieldwork produced here in Blaxhall during the mid-1970s, is a great privilege. The archive group are fortunate to have such a wealth of information, available, about so many of the past inhabitants of the village.

Rodney West
for Blaxhall Archive Group

June 2009

ACKNOWLEDGEMENTS

This project would not have been possible without the community support given during the book's development. We are greatly indebted to all Blaxhallites both past and present, too numerous to mention individually, who have contributed directly or indirectly through one way or another to its fruition. We are especially grateful to those that have given access and those who have contributed family photographs. On the same count a collective thank you goes out to all the owners of G T Rope and E M Rope artworks for allowing us to invade their privacy and photograph their treasured possessions. Thanks again go to the present owners of Ada Mannall's negatives and the permission to use the images in this book.

Thanks also go to the people and institutions that have allowed us to use images from their archives:
In particular the staff at the Henry Moore Institute, Leeds, Stephanie Boydell at Manchester Metropolitan University, Emma Roodhouse at Christchurch Mansion, Ipswich and to Dave Webster for his beautiful photographs of Ellen Mary's work at Bolton-on-Wold.

Thanks also for the assistance and help of Professors Clive Upton and Oliver Pickering and the staff of the Brotherton Library. We thank again the staff at the Ipswich branch of the Suffolk Record Office for their continuing support and invaluable help and advice. Finally, thanks to Andrew Cadman for his help with the 'mystery' of Rendlesham Camp.

CHAPTER ONE

THE GROCER'S DAUGHTER

Ada Mannall

A highlight of the project that culminated in the Archive Group's first book, 'Blaxhall's Living Past, was the 'discovery' of a cache of glass negatives containing images of Blaxhall and further afield, taken about 100 years ago. These were the work of a young woman called Ada Mannall, who was born on Stone Common in 1881. About 50 of these pictures were used in her chapter, 'The Lady Behind The Lens'. Since the book's publication and thanks to the present owners, we have scanned the remaining contents of the glass negative collection, with grateful thanks to the Ipswich branch of the Suffolk Record Office for the use of their special scanner.

Completed over several Saturdays, this scanning procedure was not a chore. Every time you placed a glass slide into the scanner and pressed the button, an image unseen for ninety years popped onto the monitor's screen. Not all were superb: some were ordinary and some were blurred (as we must remember, we are looking at Ada's complete library – warts and all.) And sometimes (sorry Ada!), because of their interest to our modern eyes, we have used a few of the not-so-perfect images.

The work of several Victorian/Edwardian photographers fill the shelves of our local bookshops but a female photographer from that period is a rare animal indeed and we feel that by giving her work a wider audience, as the first chapter in this book, we are in some way doing justice to her endeavours.

The contents of this chapter give an idea of the spread of her work but it is by no means comprehensive. One can only imagine how she organised her field trips with the need to transport camera, tripod and prepared glass negatives – well, as the locals say, she had a bike. And, by the looks of some of the photographs, she had the use of a pony-and-trap and the new-fangled motor car.

Each prepared glass negative would be carried in its own lightproof sleeve ready to be loaded into the camera. A number of her subjects contain a series of images, anything from three to five, which might suggest the sort of number she carried with her on field trips. An example of this can be seen on page 22, which shows the complete set of images dealing with 'loading the timber Jim'.

Ada's storage system. Old wooden Isinglass boxes with corrugated card stuck down two inner faces so that the negatives would be held in place. These were numbered and the inner face of the lid contained the list of the boxes contents.

That Ada knew the Rope family and in particular, Ellen Mary Rope, is reinforced by these images taken at Grove Farm. These are probably quite early photographs, definitely before 1912 as the one ABOVE shows 'Old' George Rope who died in that year. The image to the RIGHT known as 'The Gleaner' can be seen in colour on page 79 and could have been created sometime during the last years of the 19th century.

Views of Woodbridge and the River Deben by the Tide Mill, dating from the first decade of the 20th century.

ABOVE: Woodbridge Flower Show

Various views of Aldeburgh.

FAR BELOW: are members of the Mannall family and friends enjoying the seaside - note the mode of transport.

RIGHT: The Aldeburgh Golf Club with a thatched roof burned down in 1910.

Three scenes of Framlingham - the middle one labelled as 'Framlingham Pony Race'. The castle appears to be in need of some restoration.

BELOW: Ivy Lodge

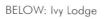

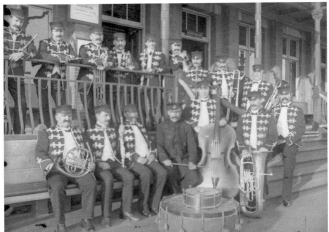

It is probably safe to assume that all these images were taken on the same visit to Lowestoft as they all come from the same storage box. We know the date as the Lowestoft Box Factory fire was in 1907. The emulsion on this particular glass negative is deteriorating though it adds to the fire effect! It is always impressive to see how Ada could get groups of individuals - usually men - to stand and pose for her photograph.

Iken Cliff. A fascinating picture which is both a historical gem and an ecological snapshot in time. Iken Cliff has been a favourite place to visit, relax and have a swim for decades - perhaps centuries.

The date of the photograph must be around the turn of the 19/20th century to judge by the fashions worn. The couple in the middle distance are standing on what appears to be a heap of material, that needed sieving, to judge be the trestle nearby. Perhaps this was coprolite dredged from the river bottom, if so this is a late date from it's use. Perhaps they are shells which had some use in the lime kiln nearby or at Iken pottery about a mile away. See also page 58 for an earlier scene of Iken Cliff.

Ecologically, there are several interesting facets. First, Ada is obviously taking the photograph from half way up the cliff face, which at this date can be seen to be fresh, loose sand - there is little open face evident today.

Most of the individuals in the portrait are standing on what appears to be a sandy beach which stretches some distance into the river - the beach structure today is very different. Finally, the river wall in the distance is complete at this date and beyond the Dunningworth Marshes stretch away towards Snape Maltings, all this is now reedbed. One of Snape's two windmills shows up faintly on the horizon.

One complete box of Ada's negatives consists of images of the military but where they were taken is a little difficult to ascertain. One clue was that on a number of her postcards she has entitled them 'Rendlesham Camp'. There appear to be soldiers from a number of regiments including the Norfolk Yeomanry. Andrew Cadman, Campsea Ashe local historian, has found a number of references in a diary from that period, he quotes: ' They came from a camp at Bealings on 31 October 1914. The Officers were billeted in Rendlesham Hall (now gone) and the men were in tents as the huts were still being built. They paraded at Ash Church every Sunday at 10.00am, usually a compliment of 200 men. The chaplain who took the service was a Reverend F Ffolkes, who was rector at Hillingdon, Norfolk. Many of the men came back for evensong and some joined the choir. The Reverend Lucas of Ash quotes - The singing was most hearty!

On the night of the 28-29 December 1914 a storm blew the field cookhouse away and damaged other buildings at Rendlesham. In January 1915 a Zepplin raid was expected and the order came round for lights out at 5pm, and this included the Army camps at Ash and Rendlesham.'

Kate Thaxton, Curator of the Royal Norfolk Regimental Museum adds this piece of information:

In the History of the Norfolk Yeomanry it says:
'In November 1914, King George V inspected the Eastern Mounted Brigade of which the Norfolk Yeomanry was a part and shortly afterwards the regiment was moved to the village of Rendlesham. Their duties during their stay in the wooden huts was to patrol the coast which they continued to do until their departure for Gallipoli in September 1915.'

The camp was at Rendlesham but the battle training area was probably under either the Bentwaters Airbase or what is now coniferous forestry.

Rendlesham Camp.

How Ada gained access would be interesting to know. Security was, presuambly, far more relaxed than today. The photograph LEFT shows Ada's parents chatting with a soldier and the background points to that meeting being on the camp grounds. The young soldier in the picture is also seen ABOVE and Ada's notes say, 'Corporal GJ Cook, 51st Durham Light Infantry. Postcard sent with Christmas card 1917.

Ada fishing along by the river between Blaxhall Hall and Beversham water mill.

Torrential rain over East Anglia during 25 and 26 August, 1912 caused much flooding.
Here the local effect can be seen at Langham Bridge, Blaxhall.

ABOVE & BELOW: Great Glemham Hall

Well Cottage, Campsea Ashe

BELOW: Little Glemham at the present A12.

CHAPTER TWO

THE BLAXHALL ARTIST

George Thomas Rope

The Family and Early Years

George Thomas Rope was the eldest son of George Rope Senior of Orford, who married Anne Pope in 1844. She lived at Grove Farm, Blaxhall where the couple set up home. The Ropes were an important local family, active in the local economy with shipping, brewing, and farming amongst their interests. George Senior achieved sufficient success to enable their eldest son, George Thomas Rope, to become an artist rather than become involved with running the farm. He was not a strong child, of weak constitution with heart trouble, and was advised to lead an easy life. It is possible the family hoped he would participate in administrative duties, and there is some evidence he assisted with accounting. The position was eased as two

George Rope Senior in a Gig outside Grove Farm, Blaxhall
Photograph 4 x 5 Private Collection.
All works illustrated are by George Thomas Rope unless indicated. Sizes where given are in inches, height before width.

brothers, younger by one and three years, were growing up with him.

Photograph - Suffolk Record Office

G.T Rope attended Ipswich School, where a photograph of his cricket team was taken, demonstrating that as a schoolboy he was not too weak to play in the 1st XI.

His school notebook, commenced in September 1859 when he was aged 13, confirms his interest in animals and his aptitude with a pen and pencil for drawing. He undoubtedly copied many drawings and Edward Lear was probably the inspiration behind the 'nonsense' drawings.

He was to remain faithful throughout his life to the subject matter in this early sketchbook, for it contains sketches of horses, fowl, farm animals, dogs, birds, rabbits and a mouse. The curious Zebra-like creature may be from a black and white engraving, as he would not have known the animal's colour, just that it bore black stripes, and

Inside front cover
and page from 1859 school sketchbook.

he assumed they were on a brown body. George studied drawing under Mr Griffin, possibly W. T. Griffiths, exhibitor at Ipswich Fine Art Club in 1875, who was later a master at Ipswich School of Art.

It may be assumed George left school in about 1864, but there is little information known about his next few years. Perhaps he went on to a form of further education, but I think the most likely sequence of events is that he remained living at Grove Farm, often visiting nearby family members whilst following his interest as a naturalist. An Almanac for 1863 contains his hand-written list of 326 British Birds, but few are ticked off, perhaps indicating he was not travelling far afield. Almost all the seabirds remain without being ticked and to my knowledge the sea held little attraction for him throughout his life. He also seems to have taken up music at this time, there are pages of music notations in the notebook, and he was known to play the 'cello with the family, his father on violin.

He kept up his sketching, recording natural history subjects and the occasional humorous drawing. Early oil paintings are not known.

It is probable that George Thomas worked in the family business on the administration side as I have an Invoice written by him to Benjamin Blunderfield in 1877. On the back is a pen and ink sketch of a spaniel. It is possible he was assigned the task of chasing debtors, as the Invoice in question is dated June and includes an outstanding account of over £15 from the previous year.

To be an Artist!

As he approached thirty years of age Young George must have been faced with a choice regarding his future career. He was obviously not disabled and he perhaps felt he should take a more active role in the family business, certainly if he wished to continue living at Grove Farm.

In 1875 there was apparently a decision to further his artistic skills, so enquiries were made in London for a place as an art pupil to William Webb, as explained in this letter:

> 25 Church Row
> Hampstead, N. W.
> March 6th, 1875
>
> Dearest Miranda
> I have ascertained that Mr. Webb will take an art pupil who is disposed to give himself to a thorough course of study although he does not, as a rule 'give lessons'. He is as you know an oil painter of standing and has of late years given himself specially to the painting of animals and bits of scenery just the subjects desired. His picture of *The Lost Sheep* created an enormous sensation in Liverpool and others of his works exhibited in the Academy have been very honourably placed on 'the line'. I say this in case Mrs. Rope may not be enough in the Art world to know what an advantage such teaching would be to her son. He is also a most delightful and cultivated man and an excellent and conscientious one, so that I feel sure that the influence and training would be splendid. He thinks the most satisfactory thing would be to see Mr. Rope and his drawings before any arrangement was made, because he might think one of the Art Schools more beneficial practice for him than any other. If he took him into his own studios he would like best to have the *entire supervision* of all his work having him at his own side all and every day – painting himself and looking at the progress made at intervals and arranging for him to take early dinner in the middle with Mrs. Webb and himself. For this arrangement Mr. Webb's terms would be for six months' study £100. Or if Mr. R. wishes to work in his own home and to come to Mr. Webb for lessons twice a week for two hours, the terms would be a guinea each lesson. The former plan would probably be much the best but a great deal would be gained by the latter.
>
> I thought it best to ask Mr Webb distinctly what his terms would be, but supposing they are not such as we thought of, Mr. Webb is so kind and helpful that he would be perfectly ready to give an opinion and advise some other artist of less standing being applied to if that were wished. His address is William Webb, Esq., 18 John Street, Hampstead. He will be much more at liberty when this month is over but still he could see Mr. Rope once and put him in the way of working sooner if time is an object with him. I think I have answered all the questions and am dearest Miranda,
>   Your loving sister
>   GERTRUDE LEWIS

LEFT: Study of a Dog, early work.
Pencil 5 x 7 Private Collection

To confirm this promotion of his career to 'Artist in Oil Paint', there is in existence another note book confirming he had training with Thomas Smythe, the Ipswich artist, either before or most likely after Webb, and possibly other local painters. The notes in this exercise book give comprehensive guides of how to achieve effects such as 'Horses at Sunset' and 'A Common Winter Sky'. The School of Art in Ipswich opened in 1881 and whilst it is possible

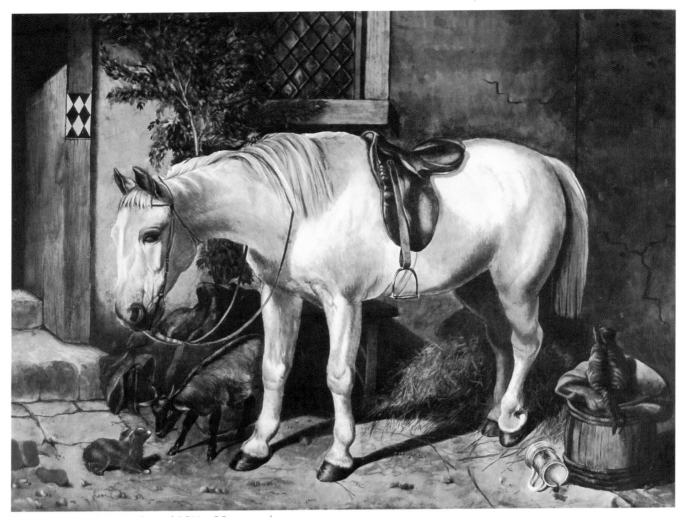

Horse outside a Cottage. Signed 19½ x 25 watercolour.
Inspired by Landseer and Herring. Private Collection.

he attended lectures there, he had by this time exhibited the 'Field Mice' at the Royal Academy, and the 'Squires Pony' in Ipswich (see Appendix 1 for a complete list of his Ipswich exhibits). These works are highly competent, so I would suggest an earlier date of the mid 1870's for his formal studies. Rope's first London exhibit was at the Royal Society of British Artists in 1876, an oil entitled 'Housed in Winter', which did not sell in London, but did sell at a later Exhibition in Suffolk.

The end of the training period with Webb marks Rope's culmination of learning from other artists and the start of his practical experience phase. Live-in training with Webb was followed by individual lessons with him, the last being recorded in G. T. Rope's expenses book on February 7th, 1877, at 10/6 per hour. In Webb's letter requesting payment he addresses George Thomas as 'Dear Mr.Rope', and passes on his wife's kind regards before finishing by asking for a Postal Order for payment, as 'country cheques can sometimes be awkward to pay away' !

London must have been an alien world to George,

A Suffolk Lane Oil

when he was there he probably missed Suffolk and his family but seems to have been well liked by the Webbs. His letters written home to Blaxhall show he took an interest in farm life and the activities of his family members, especially how the children were progressing. In 1870's London the young artist would have seen a wide variety of painting styles, with the Pre-Raphaelites still being influential but French influence starting to have an effect on the younger artists. A broader style of painting was emerging, but Rope's tutor William Webb was of the traditional school so Rope was trained to paint carefully what he observed, which undoubtedly suited his temperament as a naturalist and resulted in the production of his beautifully detailed paintings.

Success at the Royal Academy

The oil paintings from the late 1870's after his training are of outstanding quality and prove that Rope could have become a leading painter of his day, had he wished to do so. Following the sale of his small 'Field Mice' painting for 25 guineas at the Royal Academy Exhibition of 1877, he had little to prove regarding his ability as an artist to make a commercial living.

George asked William Webb's opinion of his picture at the Academy, and the letter in reply survives. After going to see it, Webb informed George the work was *'hung on the line'* which impressed him and indeed it was an honour for an unknown artist to be displayed at eye level. Consequently it was sold at the Private View as its quality could be appreciated, rather than lost with distance had it been hung two or three rows up toward the ceiling. Tactfully Webb suggested

William Webb 'Early Spring' 1856 Oil 18 x 23   location unknown

Squire's Pony. 1879 Signed Oil 17 x 23   Private Collection

some possible tonal and structural improvements. Rope preserved the Royal Academy letter stating it sold at £26.5s to David Ainsworth of Wray Castle, Ambleside, with whom he was to arrange payment and delivery.

The Ipswich Fine Art Club began holding Exhibitions in 1875, and George exhibited from 1877. Fortunately Rope's notebooks listing the majority of his output for Exhibitions have survived and these illustrate the variety of subjects he was producing. For the Ipswich Exhibition of 1877, of the eleven works, eight were oils including subjects such as Iken Cliff, Suffolk cart mare and foal, Chestnuts (illustrated here) and Field Mice, which may be the same picture as submitted to the R.A. Even more remarkably, Rope maintained a life-long ledger recording his sales of pictures, recording the buyer and price. From these it could be deduced with further research if his art 'paid its way' with sufficient works being sold to keep him in materials and enable him to travel. It must be assumed his board and lodging was provided at the various Rope Farms, perhaps he assisted with

accounts or bookwork as he had an orderly mind and neat handwriting.

There is not quite enough evidence to track his movements accurately at any stage of his life, but he shared a farm with his brother Arthur at Leiston from about 1880, confirmed by exhibition subjects. Prior to 1880 he visited Holland, resulting in a painting entitled 'At Alkmaar, Holland' exhibited in that year. His father had extensive shipping interests and it is probable the opportunity for a voyage to Holland presented itself.

Technical skills, travel and writing

From about this time onwards he experimented with works on paper, especially in pencil and wash, until he was able to capture quite remarkable effects, such as hazy days, or rising mist. His sepia and monochrome wash drawings were always competent but were further developed and are probably his most advanced form of art. Bordering on the surreal, his night scenes such as 'Something

Field Mice. Signed Oil on canvas 10 x 8. Exhibited at the Royal Academy, 1877. 25 guineas. Private Collection

Chestnuts on a mossy bank Oil on panel 6 x 8 Signed
Private Collection. Exhibited number 8, Ten guineas.

Coming' and 'At Farnham' convey a strange and
haunting atmosphere.

In 1881 he had a book published 'Sketches of
Farmyard Favourites'. Tony and Zara Webb have
located a copy in the British Museum so I now
have a facsimile copy. 22 pages describe six species,
one detailed drawing of each, followed by text.
His travels included an overseas trip to France in
1882 with his brother Edwin James Rope. A letter
home from Rouen tells his father of the Continental
agricultural methods, and enquires about family
matters. He also mentions having to return to Oisel
to finish a drawing.

Oisel, Normandy, 1882. Pencil highlighted with white 6 x 8½
signed. Private Collection

His brother Arthur, with whom he had been living
at Leiston, was married in 1883, so George moved
back to Grove Farm. He continued to travel round
England, as evidenced by his exhibits – Kent,
Surrey and in September 1883, the Lake District.
On this trip he was accompanied by his sister Ellen,
and stayed in Keswick. Perhaps he visited David
Ainsworth, purchaser of his 'Field Mice' at the
Royal Academy who lived at Ambleside. His life-
long interest in Natural History included the study
of mollusc (shells), birds and animals of all kinds,
butterflies and insects. Published work includes

articles in the various specialist journals as well
as letters on a variety of subjects. He produced
watercolours of shells for the Conchological
Society in the mid 1880's, and charged 3 shillings
6 pence for each. The discovery of many of his
manuscripts, mostly unpublished, will enable a
research project to be undertaken. Meanwhile it is
important to note he was of considerable standing
in the world of natural history, worthy of his
epitaph 'Artist and Naturalist'.

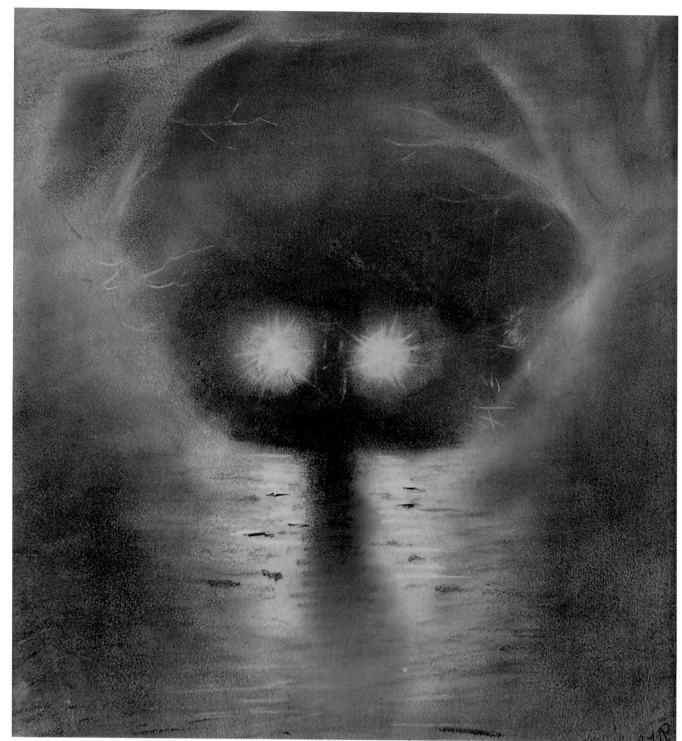

Something Coming Titled and signed, Pencil and sepia.

Snape Bridge Oil Private Collection

Snape Bridge, sketch for above oil. Pencil Private Collection

Derwent near Grange Bridge Ipswich Borough Council

Glebe Farm, Blaxhall Oil Private Collection

Langham Bridge Oil 8 x 5 Private Collection

Farm with animals. Signed Oil 16 x 22 Private Collection

From Acorn Cottage looking towards Pump Square. Signed Oil Private Collection

Cuckoo Time, Blaxhall 1888 Signed Oil Private Collection

Fresh Pastures, Hackney Mares   Signed, Oil on canvas 20 x 30 Frame inscribed Presented by Mrs Muter Ipswich Fine Art Club. 1913, Ten guineas.   Private Collection
Sold at auction in June 2000 for £4,200.

Horses on the Farm

Horses were an integral part of life at Grove Farm, and there would have been no lack of subjects on his doorstep. It has been suggested the Farm bred hackney and carriage horses, certainly many of his works feature light carriage mares and foals, and he titled works 'Hackney Mares'.

G. T. Rope constantly returns to the theme of 'Mares and Foals' and Grove Farm bred horses that were by no means a standard size and shape. I do not recall mention of the family showing any horses at Horse Fairs or Shows. Rope tried to depict individual animals accurately, even down to the pregnant mares, and named many of his subjects. His very late works are occasionally prone to inaccurate draftsmanship and perspective faults when depicting the more complex horse subjects, but his small sketches from this period are still delightful. Probably he may not have been totally happy with some works and left them in the Studio, but they have since found their way into circulation.

His exhibited works are invariably of a high standard, worked up from the hundreds of sketches he made in the field. In common with the majority of 19th century artists who worked in Suffolk, it is the 'feeling' in his pictures which comes through as the prime quality.

Sketch of a young horse - late work, Oil Private Collection

OVERLEAF - Mares and Foals. 1908 signed Oil 21 x 30   Private Collection. This is likely to be the 1908 work 'New Comers' described by Rope as 'Dk Ch cart mare and foal, grey hackney and foal'.
My father bought this circa 1965, probably from the Rope family. Illustrated in East Anglian Painters Vol.1, 1967

A Family Group, two horses and foal. Signed 1898. Sepia 11x15 Private Collection

A Family Group, two horses and foal. Pencil highlighted with white. 9 x 13 Private Collection

Horses at pasture Oil Private Collection

Horses by River. late work Signed. Private Collection

G. T. Rope's Studio at Grove Farm, Blaxhall, c.1895 Photograph 4 x 5 Private Collection

His own Studio

When he returned from living at Leiston after 1883, George no doubt had the use of a studio room at Grove Farm, but in 1889 his brother Edwin designed a Garden Studio which was built a hundred yards or so from the farmhouse.

This enabled George to have peace and quiet for his work, being ideal for painting with a good light through the window and allowing plenty of space for his specimens to assist the writing. There were also numerous framed pictures which needed accommodating and it may have been this space requirement which made George decide to have an auction of his works in Ipswich, in June 1895. Seventy-four pictures were entered and eight Plaster Casts by E. M. Rope. Most of the oil paintings sold for prices from a few pounds up to £6.15s. with the drawings averaging a guinea apiece.

The Bury St Edmunds School of Art opened in 1899 and for the inaugural Exhibition George Rope sent four oils, some of which had been shown before elsewhere, but they still give a good indication of his late 19th century style.

'Snape Street' which has lovely tones, was amongst those sent to the Bury Exhibition, as was 'November' which is an example of a countryman's painting - full of observation with a passion to capture the feeling and atmosphere of the departing day.

Churchill Babbington in his 'Birds of Suffolk' 1884, states that the Hooded Crow was, 'common on heaths', which is probably where G.T. Rope painted this bird 'around Leiston'. Very much a winter visitor, again quoted as seen in 'continuous flocks at the Corton Light Vessel flying East to West in Oct, Nov and Dec 1879'.

Snape Street, Suffolk Oil on Panel Signed 9 x 13 Private Collection

'November' Twilight Scene. Signed 14 x 20 28 guineas Private Collection

Into the 20th Century

Rope's age and eyesight may have lead to difficulties in producing highly detailed works, or perhaps he was aware of the fashion of the day, but in the early twentieth century his style changed. With broader brush strokes he became more painterly, his palette still natural with a tendency toward soft greens and strong chestnut for the horses. He was prone to deafness and photographs show him wearing glasses. At the various Exhibitions he would have seen the 'Modern British' style of painting developing, and would certainly have examined the techniques of Sir Alfred Munnings and other new wave artists. Rope's subjects after 1900 were still local landscapes, but more often with horses as part of the composition.

The major works 'Mares and Foals' (said to be at Langham Grove Farm) and 'Fresh Pastures' (Hackney Mares according to his ledger) are from circa 1908 and 1910 respectively. These works are strong and positive, indeed it is apparent that George has more confidence with the brush than at any time previously, and their size at 20' x 30' is larger than his former works. It is not unusual for an artist's style to become more fluent in later life; Arthur James Stark's working methods followed the same pattern.

A Night Journey, moonlight lane scene. Pencil and white highlight 7 x 8 Private Collection

Night – Farnham, Suffolk 9½ x 14 Private Collection. Sepia. Private Collection. Later in life, Rope worked freely with strong effects.

Mare and Foal. c.1910 Oil 16x24 Private Collection

From Snape Bridge showing old Railway Bridge Oil Private Collection

Country Sights and Sounds

Painting was absorbing less of George's time after 1910, and although he had four works in the 1915 Ipswich Fine Art Club's 41st Exhibition, some would have been painted in previous years. In May 1914 he took himself off to a farm near Nayland to stay with a family in order that he could get up at six a.m. to go out into a meadow and study some form of wildlife, tantalisingly his letter only gives that clue as to the subject. Perhaps it was related to a letter from a regular correspondent from Colchester who discussed mice with him, and made the observation George Rope knew more about the distribution of the Dormouse than anyone!

He had produced a large quantity of natural history writings and was keen to have it published. Several attempts were made to find a publisher to take it but in the end he funded the publication of 'Country Sights and Sounds' with Constable and Co. in 1915.

He paid £48 for 500 copies to be printed, and he was to receive the net proceeds from sales less 15% as their commission. It seems to have sold about half the edition, but certainly there were better times to publish a book.

The book is comprised of fifteen word sketches of subjects dealing with birds, frogs and voles but also includes an attack on corrugated iron roofing sheets which he abhorred. A sense of humour rises again in many stories, noticeably the 'Merry Porker' tale when he observes a party of young porkers being daunted by the excessive visual and vocal presence of a puffed-up turkey. However the gobbler is slowly approached by the merry band of porkers and suddenly finds his display is having no effect, so he has to retract all his extended feathers and make an exit, running off pursued by the porkers, tables turned! A letter recounting this performance was written by George to his sister.

Seventy years old in 1916, George was still in touch with his young nieces and a letter exists from Tor, the family name for the artist Margaret Edith Rope. She was a wartime farm worker in Kent and talked of being home at Leiston for twelve days on leave over Christmas. She gives him the news and sends with the letter a woodcut of a ploughing scene, which was her job. Another niece, Irene, was working in a hospital with the wounded in January 1915 and recalls enchanted visits to George's Garden Studio and walks giving great pleasure. It is said young visitors often left

3/6 Net

COUNTRY SIGHTS AND SOUNDS

BY

G. T. ROPE

LONDON
CONSTABLE AND COMPANY LTD
1915

CONTENTS

The Merry Porker. Pencil highlighted with white. 8½ x 13. No.1 Illustrating the story in 'Country Sights and Sounds'. Private Collection.

The Merry Porker. Pencil highlighted with white. 8½ x 13. No.2 Illustrating the story in 'Country Sights and Sounds'. Private Collection.

A signed oil of a scene looking towards Snape. The pencil sketch below is from nearly the same viewpoint. Private Collection

the Studio with something in their pocket, as he kept various creatures including salamanders and guinea pigs, and often had a dog about the place.

He gave his family generous gifts in the First World War period, and these, together with the printing of his book, probably indicate he had an improvement in his finances after his father died in 1912.

He invested £400 in 5% stock in 1923, whilst his Tax Assessment for 1929/30 lists his income as including 'literary work' within the income of £184, so it can be assumed he was still, at 83, submitting articles for publication.

George lived to the age of eighty-three years old following an active life, much of it spent outdoors, so the early advice to take things easy with few worries was certainly beneficial. He may well have reached his hundredth year, as did his father, had he not had an accident. From the various reports it would seem he was in a trap approaching or crossing Langham Bridge near Grove Farm when the horse took fright, possibly startled by a car, and the trap struck the boardwalk and overturned. Reportedly his heart expired two days later. The

existent manuscripts from his final years show a keen mind was still present, but thus passed a gentle man of whom it would have been an honour to make the acquaintance. Fortunately we can still know him through the evocative and sometimes intensely private paintings and drawings he left for us to enjoy.

This pencil sketch is untitled but is probably looking towards Snape from the river at Dunningworth. Signed Private Collection

Workhouse Common, Blaxhall. Signed Private Collection

A contemporary family account of his life

Extracts from hand-written notes written by one of G. T. Rope's sisters after his death, intended to be used for his obituary in 'Transactions of the Suffolk Naturalists Society' Vol. i. 1929.

'My brother was not strong when a growing man and went up to a specialist with me, his younger sister. He had heart troubles and was advised to live a quiet country life, not worrying about business or any excitements. This advice was followed and since then he has lived almost the life of a recluse taking no part in the activities of the farm either here at Blaxhall or at Leiston Lower Abbey Farm, where he lived for a time with a younger brother.'

'He became a student of nature and of art in his own way and had a studio built in the garden by his brother Edwin at Blaxhall.'

'work as an artist may be of interest to other lovers of nature especially as he so often drew or painted the smaller mammals and reptiles and made most careful and beautiful studies of them in pencil and in colour'

A Shrew Watercolour Private Collection

'There is a charming little watercolour sketch of a shrew with wonderful delicacy in the painting of the skin and fur and the curled up dead leaves surrounding it.'

'George was educated at the Ipswich Grammar School'

'He did a little drawing while there under Mr Griffen afterwards master at the School of Art but except for this he had no tuition in Art till later on'

Spaniel with Duck. Watercolour Signed 13 x 20 Private Collection Exhibited number 1, unknown exhibition.
Also illustrated: Country Life, January 1992, colour plate 1

Schoolboy sketch, March 29th 1858 Pencil & pen and ink

Obituary notes contineud:

'He had studied oil painting and worked under Mr Webb a well known painter of Eastern subjects whose son Wilfred became later secretary to the Selbourne Society.'

'After leaving Mr Webb, George painted at home and exhibited in the Royal Academy a very striking little picture of long-tailed field mice in which the form and texture both of the fur and the surroundings were wonderfully rendered. Ruskin could not have desired more faithful rending and appreciation of Nature.'

'He also went to Normandy which pleased him very much and also to Holland for a short time.'

'Having exhibited two or three times in the R. A. he definitely took up Art as a profession and took no active part in farming either here in his home or at Leiston where he had joined his brother Arthur in hiring a farm. He was not strong and was told

he must live a quiet country life, not that I think his tastes would ever have led him to choose a different kind of life.'

'When Arthur married, George returned to Blaxhall and a studio was built for him by his youngest brother Edwin, close to the house and there the rest of his life was largely spent given up to work as a naturalist and also as an artist – often painting the horses (Suffolk Punches) on the farm and sometimes painting the country round with its heath land stretching for miles towards Sudbourne and Orford and especially he loved the River Alde in it's narrow winding and reedy beds and also in its wide open reaches as at Iken'.

'He was a great lover of animals and did his best to protect them from ill treatment either intentional or unintentional (through ignorance)'

'He was a great lover of children and had many friends among them both among relatives and acquaintances. They understood and loved him well'

George Rope (senior, seated)) with some of his children. Left to right: George Thomas, the artist; Hannah Justina Lucy ("Jessie'); Edith Dorothy ('Kit'); Edwin James ('Ned'); Ellen Mary ('Nell', the sculptor), probably at the front door of Grove Farm, Blaxhall. A date for the photograph could be around 1884, which was George Rope senior's 70th birthday.

ABOVE: Evening on the Alde - near Snape Bridge. Pencil and sepia. signed.1888. 6 ½ x 9 Private Collection
Ex. Collection D. Thomas.

LEFT: The Artist Painting. Pencil Private Collection
This is from a Rope sketchbook and is almost certainly a self-portrait, he used a similar easel and is not known to have had painting companions

G. T. Rope, probably by the River Alde with his family

An oil and a pencil sketch of Iken Cliff. Featured in both these illustrations is the 'Mingay Wharfe' which was used by George Mingay then by George Rope, the elder as part of their maritime enterprise. The Mingay & Rope partnership had upwards of 12 sailing barges which plied their trade along the East Coast and the neighbouring mainland Europe ports.

The coming of the railway in the 1850s saw the end of this trade. This wharfe had completely disappeared by the time Ada Mannall took her photograph in 1900 - see page 8.

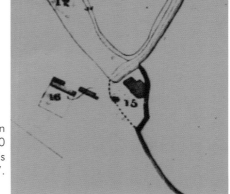

From the Iken
Tithe map of 1840
Reference 15 is
'Mingay Wharfe'.

Tabby cat stalking rabbits. Signed Pen and ink 6 ½' x 9' Given to John Day, aged 13, by his father, which started a lifelong interest in the Artist and Blaxhall.

Church Cottage, Blaxhall with the houses of Stone Common in the distance. Ada Mannall photographed the same cottage (page 16). The brick extension (right hand side) gives the cottage a unique profile - this was built on by Lord Ullswater to help accommodate the large family that lived there.

Rope's sense of humour in his art

We have found a subtle sense of humour in several of the works above, and in the description of the 'Merry Porkers'. In addition, there are many humorous stories in the notebooks. Various country topics are covered, including the story of a farmer who forgot he was getting married on a certain day and had to be rounded up on his farm to get to the church, rather late! He also recorded the local dialect in notes, which were used as a reference by George Ewart Evans when writing his book on Blaxhall, 'Ask the Fellows Who Cut the Hay' much of it based on the Ropes and Grove Farm.

Horse and Cat in a Stable, 1894 signed and dated oil 16' x 22' Private Collection The inserts show both cat and mouse in the painting - can you find them?

There was an old man of Ceylon
who traversed the deep on a swan
His appearance from land though imposing & grand
Furnished mirth for the folks of Ceylon,

LEFT: Fir Tree Farm, Blaxhall

Rope's love of cats...

Rope's lifelong obsession with mice...

Rope's hidden animals...

And to make a picture rewarding if you really look, Rope often hid a surprise, no doubt based on events that happened whilst he was painting. This would also have been to amuse children, and to encourage them to look at paintings, try them!

As with the cat and mouse in the painting, (page 61), these animals are featured somewhere, in pictures in this chapter.

ABOVE: Here is a squirrel out in the moonlight and BELOW a rabbit is rather exposed in the snow.

The Studio at Grove Farm, Blaxhall -discovering G. T. Rope's manuscripts and the recovery of E.M. Rope's works

Author's Note
This chapter was written whilst referring to a compilation of notes taken during visits to the 'Garden Studio' in 1995 and 1996. The Studio was built in 1889 for George Thomas Rope in the grounds of Grove Farm, Blaxhall, the Rope Family home, and was designed by E. J. Rope (ref: notebook by G. T. Rope). It comprises a porch, hall, a large room with fireplace, and a boarded loft above. This introduction gives the background information and is followed by extracts from my notes.

Following G. T. Rope's death 1929 the Studio was apparently used by E. M. Rope and perhaps other artistic members of the family, until finally becoming a store room. According to Robert Simper, writing in 1968, it was little used until 1963 when the family recovered about 180 canvases and drawings, some unfinished and damaged.

Acorn Cottage   Oil   Private Collection

Also evident would have been the E. M. Rope plaster casts, but in the 1960's these would have had no value, as even in the 1990's when I was handling them they had no firm commercial value, as so few had been on the market. A group of works by George Thomas were disposed of in 1963/4, probably including some of the Studio contents, to various collectors and dealers including Kenneth Moss (Springvale Collection), Cook and Harold Day of Eastbourne. Some reference material was included, much of which has since been located and is in the John Day Archive. In 1966 some works and reference material went to John Thompson (yet to be researched) Dorrie, Dorothy Anne Rope born 1883, was the family contact at that time.

I describe below my second visit when it was agreed to help the Rope Family sort through the contents of the Studio. As a result of the visit an auction of the majority of the E. M. Rope works was arranged at Bonhams in London on 26th September 1996. This had the double benefit of creating interest in E. M. Rope after many years of neglect, and raised funds to renovate the Studio building. As a direct result of the Auction the Joanna Barnes Exhibition was assembled and held at The Williamson Art Gallery in Birkenhead (22nd February 1997 to 2nd March 1997) and at Blairman and Sons in London (11th March 1997 to 27th March 1997), again bringing the Rope name to the attention of the public.

The Studio is now re-roofed and secure thanks to the efforts of Richard Rope. I am grateful to Richard and June Rope for allowing me access to the Studio and the Family reference material. As custodian of such a large quantity of material relating to George Thomas Rope it is my ambition to record and catalogue the archive, and produce a catalogue raisonné of his works that I have seen and recorded over the years

Following my first visit to the somewhat derelict little building in the garden of Grove Farm, it certainly whet my appetite to go back for extended visits to catalogue and tidy up the contents to see what might be found. It was an exciting project, as recorded below in the notes I made at the time....

The Garden Studio, as I first saw it in 1995

With the knowledge that there were more treasures to be unearthed, following the first brief look, another visit was planned with a view to making a more thorough search. The early explorers of the Pyramids must have had a similar thrill of anticipation!

Having gained access with a member of the Rope family, a satisfying couple of hours were spent rummaging amongst the contents of the Studio.

My search was rewarded by the uncovering of a quantity of oil sketches, many studies of animals and a few landscapes. One or two were so black with dust and grime that the subjects were unrecognizable. A few drawings were discovered in broken frames and will be transformed by careful cleaning. The oil of the sitting hen was a dark, almost black panel with nothing discernible. Careful time-consuming cleaning revealed a fine work.

On my previous visit to the studio I had been interested to see huge piles of paperwork and notes, much of it in G. T. R's handwriting. The earliest books were found to cover farm accounts going back to the 1820's and made interesting browsing looking at the corn and produce prices. The Rope Family owned a quay at Iken and shipped produce to London and the North of England. Amongst other books was an English - French dictionary which explained a lengthy essay by G. T. R. written or copied in French, some of it quite technical. He is thought to have visited France only once in 1882 which produced a number of drawings including 'On the Seine' and a view at Oisel.

Returning to the manuscripts, much of the material was found to relate to G. T. Rope's articles about birds, cats and wildlife, much of it published in the natural history journals of the day. He is known to have produced many pamphlets and at least two book titles were published, one in 1881 and 'Country Sights and Sounds' in 1915.

Study of a chicken.   Oil on board 9x11 Private Collection

Interior of the studio, E.M. Rope sculptures together with G. T. Rope's notes, specimens, oils and drawings

A selection of E.M.Rope sculptures I arranged for a photograph in 'as found' condition. Lower left is an important work 'Marigold - A Gleaner' circa 1900 which is a true Blaxhall inspired subject (see page 79).

A couple of expanding files were discovered, one containing a number of letters, and the other sundry manuscripts. Further investigation will reveal the exact contents, but it was exciting to find the Royal Academy receipt for the picture of mice exhibited in 1877 and the sale details for the not inconsiderable sum of £26.10. Also revealed was his tax return for 1929/30 which had lain undisturbed for 65 years.

My next visit to the Studio in 1995 was to assess the works by George Rope's sister, E. M. Rope, a sculptor, mainly in plaster, working early in the 20th Century. The studio had been used as a store for her work and it was interesting to find photographs of commissions which had been completed. Quite how the plaster casts were made will have to be researched as there were a number from the same cast. The larger works appear to be hand crafted as sculptures. No moulds were discovered, perhaps they were cast elsewhere and finished by hand in E. M. Rope's studio, which was located in London.

When it is considered that the majority of her output was incorporated into buildings or memorials, it is remarkable to find such a large number of works by a sculptor such as E. M. Rope still undisturbed

in one place. The war was less forgiving to fragile plaster works, and bronze was often salvaged for the war effort, along with other metals.

The Collection discovered at the Studio includes some of the Royal Academy works which were returned to Blaxhall from E. M. Rope's Chelsea studio. Many have labels and signatures and most are in dirty untouched condition. The plaques were originally presented in wooden frames, and when displayed offer an unusually decorative feature, reflecting the changing styles of the period 1880 - 1920.

The subjects for the commissioned works are often religious and sombre, but Ellen's personal productions are based upon the themes of children, fairy stories and the countryside. There is little doubt that she was influenced by growing up on a working farm with her older brother George Thomas Rope, who was both an artist and naturalist.

During my visit I took a number of photographs and set about researching options to be considered for the E. M. Rope works. They were certainly in need of preservation. Values of her work were difficult to obtain, but I considered that a well publicised auction in London would be the best option, and proposed one be held in 1996.

In spring of 1996 Richard Rope and I listed the E. M. Rope works and a van was arranged to take them to London, where I worked with the auctioneers to ensure they went in a suitable sale. An Architectural Antiques and Sculpture sale was chosen which which was successful as the sale attracted several serious buyers, from London's West End and elsewhere.

The George Thomas Rope Archive

We are very fortunate in having a considerable reference source to enable an insight into the life and times of G. T. Rope. Many famous artists have a good pool of information available, Constable has nine volumes of correspondence and countless books and catalogues to refer to. Turner also has a huge number of references available.

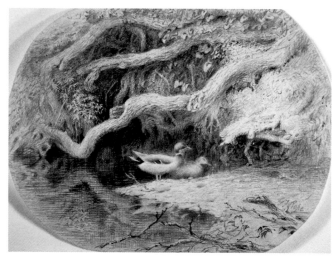

Ducks under a bank. signed pencil Private Collection.

What is remarkable in this case is that G .T .Rope is not a world-renowned artist and yet so much has survived. We can use this to get to know the man and understand his art. It is beyond the scope of this chapter to explore in depth, but references are made to some of the Archive in the text above, and more are to be found in the following paragraphs, taken from notes made during further visits to the Studio after the auction of E. M. Rope's sculptures.

Over the previous few months the studio had been given a new roof, a rebuilt chimney stack and renovated windows. This work has ensured that the building will survive in sound order for the future. The interior is still in fairly original order, with many of G. T. Rope's cabinets and fittings. His easel, a folding portable wooden version, is stored in the studio.

Whilst the renovations were being undertaken, a quantity of archive material was recovered from the roof and cabinets.

The most interesting are approximately 20 sketchbooks, even though the majority have had leaves removed or mutilated by the cutting out of the studies. The remaining drawings will provide an insight into his method of working. For instance it is apparent that he desisted from the extensive use of a rubber, as it would seem that if something did not please him he evidently left it and started afresh.

Another source of reference will be a large number of paid invoices he retained from tailors, grocers and artists colour-men. These reveal a neat mind, and serve to indicate the materials he consumed, including canvasses and frames.

It has previously been suggested that G. T. Rope used inferior paints and materials, leading to a

A Sketchbook, as used by G.T.Rope, Private Collection. Stored since his death in the Artist's Studio at Blaxhall.

deterioration of his works. In my opinion this is a misinterpretation of the results of poor after-care of many of his works. He was guilty of not always varnishing his works to seal and protect them after the paint was fully dry, normally after three to six months. The cleaning of his works in all mediums demands the utmost care, and experience is essential to understand paint reactions and surface textures. Rope trained under William Webb in London and would have been familiar with contemporary techniques. He also had instruction early on from Thomas Smythe of Ipswich, who at the time used quality materials. From Rope's receipts we know he did not scrimp on materials, and often paid well for framing his works, indicating a pride and interest in their presentation.

The remaining papers include many photographs and engravings of various breeds of horses,

Paintings and a drawing from Ellen Mary's early years.
TOP LEFT: a portrait of her nephew Bill Toller as a young boy
(also in the source photograph).

Drawing by Ellen Mary Rope, courtesy of Linda Taylor (found loose in a book).

ABOVE: Sketch 'Mother and Child'
BELOW: Plaster panel on a typical Ellen theme.

George Rope Senior, Ellen's father.
Plaster Cast 8 x 6.5 Private Collection

LEFT: Panels over a fireplace in her brother Arthur's farmhouse.
see Appendix 2.
BELOW: Certificate gained by Ellen Mary at the Slade.

LEFT: Bellringer

woman artists:
'.. the art of the sculptor in its noblest form demands strenuous labour so that you may regard it as being tolerably secure from invasion by the new woman or the mere dilettante; for it is a most perfect instance of fine art inextricably allied with fine craft'. [5]

Susan Beattie adds: 'Among the first 'new women' to reach for precisely that alliance of sculptural art and craft was Ellen Mary Rope'. In other words, as a woman sculptor towards the end of the Victorian period, Ellen Mary was something of a pioneer. Similarly, the Women's Studies Encyclopaedia mentions her name and immediately afterwards adds this:

'The history of Victorian women artists is not one of unalloyed and unimpeded progress. Although women were increasingly admitted to art schools, they were segregated within these institutions .... This sexual differentiation also occurred when artists set up in professional practice and attempted to establish a reputation and make a living from their work. .... Exhibiting organizations, dealers, and galleries also often discriminated against women; even by the late nineteenth century only 10 per cent of the work at major exhibitions was created by women.'[6]

In an early interview (ironically for 'Woman at Home' magazine), Ellen Mary herself was not optimistic about the prospects for a woman sculptor, concluding: 'Sculpture is not a very hopeful 'women's employment'.[7]

One thing that did help women artists of the time was co-operation and solidarity among themselves and with other progressive women. Ellen's early association with Octavia Hill remained an important contact and was reinforced by growing links within the Garrett circle[8], as well as her close collaboration with Elinor Hallé. These links must have provided important encouragement as well as the source of commissions (see below). A glimpse of the workings of this mutual support comes from the history of a younger woman sculptor, S. R. Praeger, who started at the Slade in 1888 and soon became a part of the same circle and a particular friend of Ellen's. Despite returning to Ireland and pursuing her career there, the

Drawing of Ellen Mary Rope in her later years by Sophia Rosamond Praeger

connection between the two remained strong and drew in other artists, both Irish and English.[9] Their artistic careers have many parallels and as late as 1929 Praeger drew Ellen's portrait, see above.

Sculpture at the period was in the process of breaking free of the stylistic conventions of late neo-classicism in favour of a more naturalistic approach. As emphasised by the ideology of the Slade when it opened: '[the] study of the living model... [is] ...of first and paramount importance'.[10] Added to this was an admiration of the Italian tradition of, for example, Luca Della Robbia and his successors within the same family. It was therefore thoroughly consistent that Ellen Mary should join the Della Robbia Pottery of Birkenhead as one of its most significant female designers, working for them from around 1896 until its closure in 1906. The rationale of the Pottery drew not only upon the eponymous Italians' style but also on the ideals of the Arts and Crafts movement, in which Ellen Mary was firmly located. Her association with the Pottery may have come about partly as a result of being a contemporary at the Slade of Harold Rathbone, Della Robbia's moving force. Her typical works were relief panels in a variety of materials and featuring human figures, particularly children or mother figures with children. She also favoured themes involving the sea – waves and sea-creatures often in fanciful roles, for example children riding sea horses or dolphins through the surf.

[5] quoted in Beattie (1983), p. 196
[6] Women's Studies Encyclopaedia, p. 192
[7] Woman at Home (1895), p. 477
[8] Crawford (2002), pp. 288 - 292

[9] McBrinn (2007), pp.16,18,20,26
[10] Beattie (1983), p.14

Four views of a tea caddy by Ellen Mary Rope

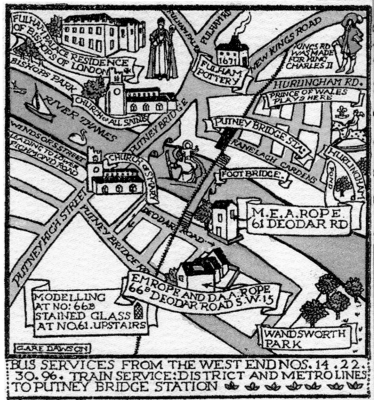

ABOVE: Putney map showing studio locations of Ellen Mary and her nieces.

BELOW & BACKGROUND: Letter from Ellen Mary to her nephew, Harry Rope, describing life in Putney.

RIGHT: Watercolour by Margaret Rope the Younger: view across the Thames from her studio.

[Shortly after the elder Margaret Rope, 'Marga', had become a nun in 1923, her cousin Margaret Rope the younger, 'Tor', moved to Putney. Both were stained glass artists and one of them made the porch window at St Peter's, Blaxhall, to an Ellen Mary Rope design.] At the time, Ellen wrote to her nephew Harry: '… *I am glad to hear our Margaret's window is so rightly appreciated at Birkenhead. I thought myself it was one of her most successful windows especially from a decorative point of view. Tor misses her still very sadly. She is going to move out of the Lettice Street studio at Xmas into a new one in the house of friends at Putney - a beautiful studio with a fine view of the Thames opposite Hurlingham where their own garden runs down to the river and there is a splendid outlook on sky and water & now & then a heron finds its way to the shore and ducks of many hues swim round about but she feels very sorry to leave her old room which is full of reminiscences of happy times with Marga. My dear kind girls here are always thinking and doing for me & I feel a greatly spoiled Aunt but I was very tired when I came back, because of the nursing and house running at home, and I am now beginning to feel almost normal again.'*

Polychrome panels

TOP: 'Water Babes', courtesy of Robin Fanshawe
ABOVE: 'Marigold, a Gleaner'

The spirit of her work fits comfortably within the Arts and Crafts Movement, itself part of the heritage of the Pre-Raphaelite Brotherhood and associated to some extent with Art Nouveau. In the Movement, pride in craftsmanship was emphasized, as well as affordability. To modern eyes, some examples of the style may appear to be rather innocent, even sentimental, but in its time it was a step forward into modernity. Ellen's involvement with the Movement can be seen in her participation at each Arts and Crafts Exhibition Society show from 1889 onwards. She exhibited panels for ceiling, wall, mantelpiece and nursery decoration as well as designs for practical everyday objects: an electrical bell push, doorplates, a tea caddy and a letterbox. She is said to have aimed to be accessible to people of relatively modest means: her panels 'were primarily designed to be executed at a low cost and repeated if desired, so that they could be used by others than the very rich.' [11]

Among the other sculptors she came into contact with through the Movement was Robert Anning Bell, a leading exponent of painted plaster relief. Ellen Mary herself was of course also producing panels in this medium, one example being 'Marigold, a Gleaner' - a portrait of a girl in a harvest field. This work overlapped with her design work for Della Robbia and these small plaster panels, whether painted or not, became the genre for which she was particularly recognised.

On a completely different scale to her domestic pieces, Ellen Mary was also involved in large

[11] The Builder (3rd December 1898), p. 508

Major commission for Rotherhithe Town Hall Council Chamber: 20 foot long plaster bas-relief illustrating life on the Thames in 1700, sadly destroyed in the Second World War. All that survives is the distressed photograph above (part of the Henry Moore Institute archive on Ellen Mary) and the design (below) from the article on her work in 'The Builder', 3rd December, 1898.

PLASTER PANEL 20 ft. LONG IN COUNCIL CHAMBER, ROTHERHITHE TOWN HALL "DOCKS AND TIMBER TRADE IN THE THAMES IN THE YEAR 1700" VESTRY ARMS IN CENTRE

A SEA-CHARIOT. (EXHIBITED AT THE SALON IN BRONZE, 1897; ROYAL ACADEMY, 1898.)

DESIGN FOR OVER-MANTEL. (ROYAL ACADEMY, 1898.)

PORTRAIT RELIEF OF FOUR CHILDREN. (NEW GALLERY 1898.)

A SEA-CHASE. DESIGN FOR OVER-MANTEL. (ROYAL ACADEMY, 1897.)

ABOVE: Further illustrations from 'The Builder' article, 1898: a number of plaster panels.
BELOW: 'Angel with Trumpet', design for the head of a column in St. Peter's, Cricklewood

The Alexandra Hall in Morley Town Hall, Leeds

The black and white photographs are from 1921 and show the three large panels (detail: see inset), 'Faith, Hope and Charity' by Ellen Mary in the Alexandra Hall, Morley Town Hall, Leeds. As the contemporary colour photograph shows, they have been unfortunately replaced.

'The four spandrels Faith, Hope, Charity and Heavenly Wisdom, originally made for Women's Building at the World Exposition in Chicago 1893, were later installed in the Chenies Street Chambers Ladies Residential Dwellings, a London residence for professional single or widowed women.' The one illustrated her is 'Hope'.

BELOW: Postcard from the World Exposition 1893 showing the Women's Building where Ellen Mary's four spandrels decorated the vestibule.

ABOVE RIGHT: The Ladies' Residential Chamber in Chenies Street - illustrated in 'The Builder' 1889.

RIGHT: Chenies Street Chambers at it is today.

The original space has now been divided into separate rooms but the wingtips can still be seen protruding from beyond the new wall.

architectural work, which was an important aspect of 'The New Sculpture'. In her 'Woman at Home' interview, she had expressed the ambition 'to work for architects, and to decorate the outside of houses'.[12] Her Della Robbia design work brought her into more public view and this, together with her role within the Arts and Crafts Movement, led to commissions for works of sculpture that were designed to be incorporated into buildings. 'The transformation of architectural carving and modelling from anonymous, scarcely noticed craft to dynamic, seductive art was the greatest collective achievement of the New Sculptors and one of the most rational expressions of Arts and Crafts ideals in nineteenth-century history.'[13] Among the architects for whom she worked were Arnold Mitchell, Horace Field and I. Goodison – but, alas, despite its significance at the time, little of this work survives today.

In 1893, the World Columbian Exposition was held in Chicago and for the first time at such an event there was a specific Women's Building. The time was critical – two of the United States had already granted female suffrage – so, unsurprisingly, the establishment of this special building designed and operated by women was controversial. Ellen Mary was honoured to receive a commission to design four spandrels (panels to be set beside an arch) for the British section of the building. Each polychrome plaster relief was nearly six feet tall, representing Faith, Hope, Charity and Heavenly Wisdom. After the Exposition closed, there were competing claims for these panels. They were sought by the newly-established South London Gallery, Camberwell, but they had already been sold elsewhere. Octavia Hill, Ellen's early teacher at Nottingham Place School, had acquired them for a project in central London, off Goodge Street. Chenies Street Chambers Ladies Residential Dwellings (1888) was one of a number of similar initiatives undertaken by the small circle of practical socialists including not only Hill but also Dr. Elizabeth Garrett Anderson (Britain's first woman doctor), her sister Agnes Garrett and other professional women and suffragettes who lived in Bloomsbury in the 1880s. It was a building of purpose-built flats, designed to provide homes for professional single or widowed women who wanted not only a safe dwelling-place but also a like-minded community of educated, artistic women. Ellen's panels were installed in the basement in a room used as a dining hall. Unfortunately, the panels are now largely lost to view. Two of the four ('Hope' and 'Charity') remain, incorporated into subdivided spaces but the other two were taken out during dry rot treatment in the 1970s and are rumoured to have been placed on a skip. The tips of two angels' wings are still visible in a hallway.[14] 'Hope' also lives on as the cover illustration for Elizabeth Crawford's important study referred to earlier.

Other architectural commissions from this period included bas-reliefs for the Women's University Settlement in Nelson Square, Southwark, based on Chaucerian quotations and commissioned by Octavia Hill. Ellen Mary also made three large female figures in plaster representing Faith, Hope & Charity for the magnificent Morley Town Hall near Leeds, probably commissioned by a local suffragist, Alice Cliff Scatcherd. The figures stood high on one end wall of the Alexandra Hall and, judging from contemporary photos, must each have been over seven foot high. Unfortunately, they have since been removed, at some time after 1921, and their fate has not been traced. Another work, from around 1901, a pair of panels for the chapel of the East Anglian (TB) sanatorium at Nayland, Suffolk, another project of members of the Garrett circle, was lost when the chapel was deconsecrated[15]. Largest of all these architectural commissions was a panel for Rotherhithe Town Hall - but again it has been lost, in this case destroyed in the Second World War. Only basic images survive as testimony to its extent and intricacy. Twenty feet in length and cast in plaster, this ambitious piece set out to illustrate the history of the shipping and timber trades associated with the River Thames in 1700. To achieve authenticity of detail, Ellen Mary prepared for the work by visiting shipyards and wharves along London's riverbanks and by consulting archive illustrations in South Kensington Museum.[16]

Apart from secular architectural creations, she also produced works intended for church decoration, often through the Church Crafts League, an offshoot of the Arts and Crafts Exhibition Society, frequently in the form of memorials. For example, in 1905-06 she made a series of reliefs in cement for St Mary's, Bolton-on-Swale, in memory of Admiral Talbot Carpenter and his wife. Other examples of her work for churches can also be seen in Cricklewood (St Peter's), in Aldershot (St Joseph's) and Merton, Norfolk (St Peter's) – as well as those closer to her Suffolk home, which are described later. The series at Aldershot is particularly notable, including seven plaster panels, white on a gold background.

[12] Woman at Home (1895), p. 477
[13] Beattie (1983), p. 6
[14] Chenies Street Chambers Historical Society website
[15] Probably entitled 'Palm Sunday Children' or 'Benedictus Qui Venit in Nomine Domini', one panel being of the same design as the bronze panel in Ipswich Museum
[16] Kendall (1899), p. 209

St. Joseph's Church, Aldershot, Hampshire

LEFT: St. Joseph's Chuch, Aldershot contains an impressive range of panels by Ellen Mary made expressly for the church at the time of its original construction.

BELOW: A memorial for her brother Henry, a much respected Shropshire doctor, in St. Mary's, Shrewsbury: design and execution.

RIGHT: One of Ellen Mary's many First World War memorials, this one to Herbert Lyttelton Pelham.

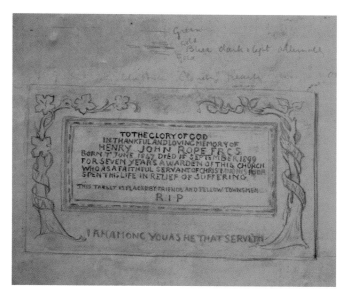

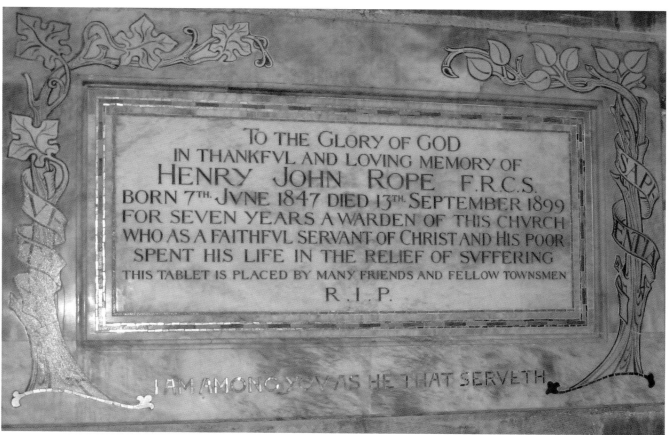

Ellen Mary's handwritten notes (see right)
'... a modelled decoration in ivory tinted cement
covering the walls of a small chapel in memory
of Admiral Talbot Carpenter, Bolton-on-Swale
church....' She then quotes text drawn from
Psalm 104 and incorporated in the design.

Bolton-on-Swale, Yorkshire

At the very end of the nineteenth century, Ellen Mary had a more personal commission when she lost the second of her brothers to die at an early age. In 1874, Richard Frederick had died aged 22 as a result of a diving accident, when Ellen Mary was just 19. Then, in 1899, her brother Henry John, a doctor working in Shrewsbury, died at the relatively early age of 52. In response, Ellen Mary produced two memorials, one a coloured plaster triptych to be placed in Shrewsbury Children's Hospital, and another in stone, a wall plaque for St Mary's, Shrewsbury, where Henry John had been a churchwarden. Nor was this the last family bereavement she was called on to commemorate: late in her life she contributed a panel for the chapel (now church) built in memory of Henry John's youngest son, Michael, at Kesgrave, near Ipswich.[17]

Around the turn of the twentieth century, from 1903 in fact, she started sharing a studio (first in Devonshire Mansions, Marylebone Road, later at 404c Fulham Road) with her niece Dorothy Anne Aldrich Rope, then aged 20, who became first her student and later co-worker, adopting much of her style and many of her motifs. When the First World War interrupted the gentle tenor of life, another strand of Ellen Mary's work developed, namely memorials, either for individuals or for the fallen of a school or a parish. One particular design ('The Angel of the Resurrection') was especially popular, being used at Stone House School, Broadstairs (the memorial is now relocated), at Pietermaritzburg, South Africa and elsewhere. (The design portrays an angel with trumpet by its side, lilies in the foreground, sunrise over the sea in the background.) In fact, memorials occupied much of her productive effort from 1917 until the mid-1920s and beyond, so much so that during this time she largely refrained from submitting work to exhibitions. She was by then, of course, approaching normal retirement age. Nevertheless, she continued to work well into her seventies, assisted by her niece Dorothy, and living close to the studios of two other nieces who worked as stained glass artists in Putney, southwest London. As late as Christmas 1931, she was sending her nephew Harry Rope a picture of a panel she had completed for Masasi Cathedral, East Africa 'in which I have made Our Lady and the Holy Child rather dark in complexion by request of the Bishop who is keen on making the Africans feel the Christian religion is for all races and not in any way European as the representations of a fair English Holy Family are apt to suggest'.[18] Other letters from this time show that even in her seventies she felt torn between her artistic life in the city among her nieces, whom she called her 'dear girls', and her home back in Blaxhall (see page 78). However, in her final years, she spent progressively more and more time at Grove Farm, finally dying there at the age of 79.

Assessment

The history of the reputation of Ellen Mary Rope as an artist is one of recognition and acclaim in her time, succeeded by a period of obscurity and anonymity, followed at the very end of the twentieth century with a revival of interest and appreciation.

Any assessment of an artist who has suffered a posthumous eclipse has the potential to be controversial: perhaps the safest route is first to return and view them in the light of their own times. This is what two contemporary writers said about her:

'Her realm is the land of legend and romance, peopled by 'fairy beings sweet and pure' – delicious little lads and maidens, children of the sea, half mortal, half immortal, rollicking cupids and solemn-faced angelini. Miss Rope is an ideal sculptor of little children; she reproduces to perfection the dainty roundness of their limbs, their artless grace of gesture, their expression of innocent mischief or limpid candour. For them she becomes a child again, she enters into all their joys and griefs because she loves them and she glories in portraying their fresh beauty' [19]

'Her attention has for the most part been devoted to small decorative works in relief, and her work in this direction is marked as much by charming fancifulness of conception and design as by a high degree of skill in execution. The delightful little panels of children …are perhaps better known than her more serious works, but they alone are sufficient to accord her a place in the ranks of our decorative sculptors. Simple and graceful in style, they remind one sometimes of the Della Robbias, by reason of the beauty and simplicity of the child-forms' [20]

Yet the qualities admired in her time are those that some contemporary critics find hardest to appreciate: ' … these often overly sentimental images create within us a struggle to take them

---

[17] See 'Where her works are', see p. 95
[18] Correspondence of Ellen Mary Rope in the Suffolk Record Office archives HA 412/1/1/6; see also page 96.

[19] Kendall (1899), p. 209
[20] 'A.F.' (1900), p. 323

The assured mature artist

seriously, tempted as we are to dismiss them as little more than kitsch'.[21] But the same author goes on to recognize that Ellen Mary could span a range of styles from the Pre-Raphaelite poetic spirit to the strikingly realistic, and concludes:

'The fluidity with which [Ellen Mary] Rope approached her career enabled her to adapt to the market and thus sustain a comfortable living as a sculptor and decorative artist. She exhibited widely and internationally, and received considerable

respect in the art press of the day. That she achieved professional status and continued to produce her time-honoured designs well into the 20th century reveals a considerable aptitude for reading her market. More than just another notable woman sculptor, Ellen Mary Rope was a manifold product of her time.'[22]

And then, as the twentieth century ended, the catalogue accompanying the 1997 retrospective exhibition offered this reassessment of Ellen Mary Mary Rope's achievement:

[21] Darling-Glinski (2003) p. 303

[22] ibid, p. 304

'Based on the evidence of the recently discovered corpus of her work and the details of her career, Rope appears eminently worthy of the accolades she received from contemporary writers. But more than that, Ellen Mary Rope is revealed as an artist who successfully combined a delicate sensitivity and considerable technical skill with a lively imagination and intellect. Her work is a lasting testimony to this achievement.'

As we have seen, Ellen Mary herself was quoted as seeing the chances of success for a woman sculptor in her day to be distinctly limited. And yet, within a very few years, she was established as a sculptor who was proficient in a variety of styles and media and who could support herself by her art. If sometimes her works border on the sentimental or popular, this is simply a reflection of the taste of the time and an indication that Ellen Mary knew her market. When opportunity and a discerning patron allowed, her art could achieve more sublime levels.

A further question remains: how far might we describe Ellen Mary as a 'modern woman'? At the distance of almost a century, we may assume from her professional associates, for example Octavia Hill, her educational background at the Slade and her achievements in a male-dominated world, that she must have had some inclination towards feminism, as we would now call it. As we have seen, she was an active member of the Garrett circle of artists, thinkers and social reformers. As a slight counterbalance, we may weigh these words from a letter to her nephew, the distinguished Roman Catholic priest and author, Father H.E.G. Rope:

'…. There was one thing in your former letter that I always wanted to contradict but it seemed so comic that I could not believe you really thought it i.e. that Dorry [Ellen's niece and student, Dorothy] was such a suffragette! Of course like most women who have thought much about it she felt as I do that women should have their say in what concerns them and children but it is not at all a strong point with her and she was certainly not a militant which is what is meant generally by suffragette. She is a dear good brave helpful girl full of resource and sweet unselfishness, always thinking far more about her brothers and sisters than herself….'[23]

We need to allow for the fact that the recipient was a conservative Catholic priest with a strong vein of nostalgia for pre-industrial Britain[24] – for him even the bicycle was something of an abomination! We should also note that she only disowns the epithet 'militant' for her niece.

Ellen Mary was certainly among the 'new women' of sculpture in her time and mixed in progressive circles: for example, we find her name listed in Woman's Leader, published by National Union of Women's Suffrage Societies in 1918. Although her interests focused on her art, especially the representation of children and of subjects from classical mythology and biblical stories, Ellen Mary should also be seen as very much *au courant* with the thinking of her times and, artistically at the very least, keen to advance the cause of women.

Where her works are

Although Ellen's works are dispersed around Britain and abroad (as far afield as South Africa) some still remain close to her Blaxhall base – in private homes, but also more publicly in churches: in St Peter's, Blaxhall; at Little Glemham, Leiston, Aldeburgh, Stowupland and Kesgrave - as well as at Ipswich Museum, but not normally on public view there.

Two of her most accessible designs are in Blaxhall church: the windows in the porch and the panel of an angel holding a child with a palm, in a window opening on the north side. The windows were derived from a design by Ellen Mary but almost certainly made by one of her nieces, both of whom were named Margaret Rope, and who were practising artists in stained glass within the Arts and Crafts tradition. The windows show her typical cherubic children's faces and a decorative lettering style unlike the more classical lettering favoured by her nieces. Inside the church, in a window aperture in the north wall, the painted plaster angel and child panel ('The Guardian Angel') is entirely Ellen's work and is an excellent example of her particular qualities, consummate technique, sensitive portrayal and an empathy with the themes of innocence and gentleness.

But there is more. Further back along the same north wall in Blaxhall parish church is the war memorial plaque, designed and made by Ellen Mary. Inevitably more austere and solemn, the bronze panel portrays Christ leaning down to raise the hand of a fallen soldier, with weapons of war on either side. It is also worth noting the style and excellence of technique in the lettering below. Also along the north wall at the east end is an engraved stone memorial, in memory of the son of

[23] Correspondence of Ellen Mary Rope in the Suffolk Record Office/Ipswich archives HA 412/1/1/6
[24] see Rope (1931)

ABOVE: Memorial tryptych to Henry John Rope, Ellen Mary's brother originally in Shrewsbury's Children's Hospital, incorporating designs used elsewhere. The lefthand panel echoes one from Blaxhall Church (see page 92). The righthand panel, 'Mother and Child', was a design originally created for Della Robbia, see RIGHT.

(The tryptch is now relocated in the main corridor of Shrewsbury Hospital.)

Ernest Bates, the then rector. The boy was Alfred Aldrich Bates and he died in 1904 at the age of 6. Appropriately, the image is of a protective angel taking a small child by the hand. The same north wall also carries a panel in memory of Marjorie Wilson, daughter of the then vicar Cameron-Wilson, but this was by Dorothy Rope. Also in the church are crib figures, rare examples - albeit small ones - of sculptures in the round by Ellen Mary.

In other churches close to Blaxhall are more works by Ellen Mary. At Little Glemham (St Andrew's), there is a panel 'Laborare est orare' (Work is prayer), moved here from the village hall. At Leiston, where her brother Arthur was a farmer, Ellen Mary contributed a charming coloured plaster panel for the Children's Corner of St Margaret's church. Close by, at Aldeburgh (St Peter & St Paul), is Ellen's memorial (Fides, Spes, Caritas) to the 'mater familias' of the Garrett clan, Louisa Garrett née Dunnell. A little further afield is St Michael and the Holy Family, Kesgrave, a church originally conceived as a memorial to a nephew of Ellen's, Michael Rope, an aeronautical engineer, who died in 1930 in the catastrophic crash in northern France of the airship R101.[25] Here, outside Ipswich, near her family home, his widow Doreen Lucy née Jolly established a church

in his memory and filled it with works of art by his relatives. Ellen's contribution is the plaster panel over the doorway: 'Ecce Agnus Dei', depicting the Virgin and Child and a lamb, but also a young boy, perhaps symbolising Michael Rope in his youth. One further local church, this time north of Ipswich, Stowupland Holy Trinity, has work by Ellen Mary: the small war memorial located on the wall to the right of the chancel.

It is quite possible that people reading this chapter have seen Ellen's work or may even possess an example, perhaps without knowing it. Much of her sculptural activity used methods of casting that allowed some, even many, copies to be made and in various materials, e.g. metals, plaster etc. There are several cases where the same design is known to appear in a number of different places. For example, the angel and child from Blaxhall church reappears in Ellen's memorial triptych to her brother Dr Henry John Rope, displayed at The Shrewsbury & Telford Hospital NHS Trust. The same triptych also contains a panel that was used elsewhere as a design for the Della Robbia Pottery. Another version of this whole piece appeared for sale by auction in 2004 and more may be extant. The same must be true of many of her other designs.

25 see page 102 for a contemporary letter written by Ellen Mary

St. Peter's Church, Blaxhall, Suffolk

Several pieces of Ellen Mary's work can be seen in her local church of St. Peter's, Blaxhall.
LEFT: 'The Guardian Angel'

LOWER LEFT: Memorial to Alfred Aldrich Bates - who, tragically, died very young.

LOWER RIGHT: The village First World War memorial in bronze.

OPPOSITE PAGE: Two-light stained glass window in the porch by Margaret Rope, her niece, to a design by Ellen Mary.

St. Andrew's Church, Little Glemham, Suffolk

St.Margaret's Church, Leiston, Suffolk

Other pieces of Rope family art can be seen at St. Margaret's, Leiston, including nativity figures and a polychrome panel, originally for the Children's Corner, by Ellen Mary and a memorial to the younger Arthur Rope, executed by Dorothy Rope, her niece, student and assistant. Arthur George Michael Rope, Dorothy's brother, died at school in Canterbury in his mid-teens.

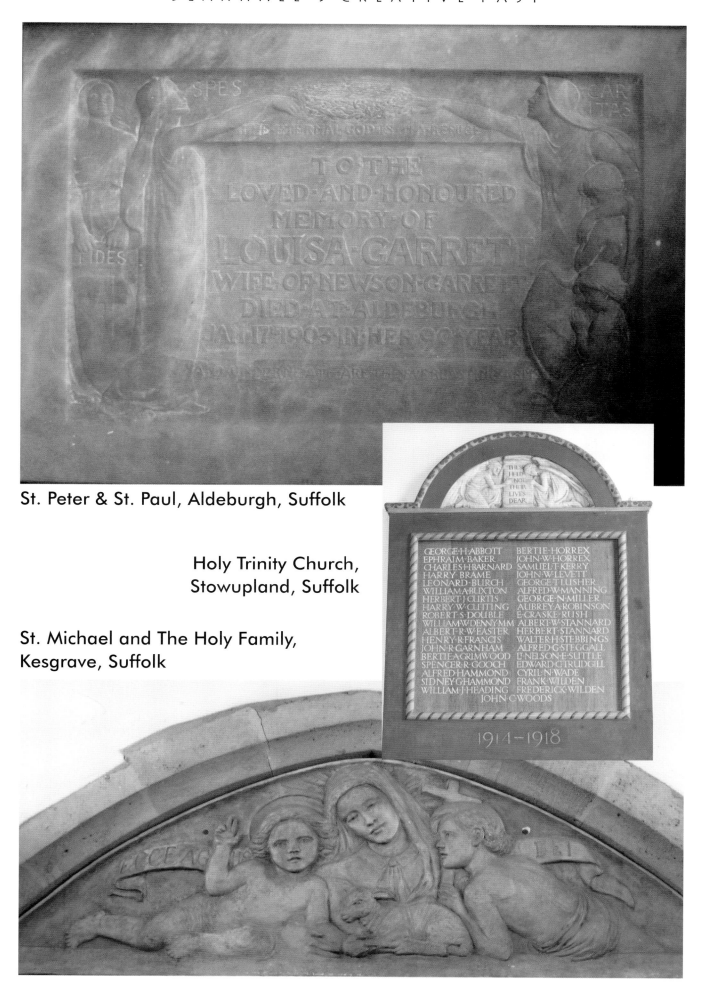

St. Peter & St. Paul, Aldeburgh, Suffolk

Holy Trinity Church,
Stowupland, Suffolk

St. Michael and The Holy Family,
Kesgrave, Suffolk

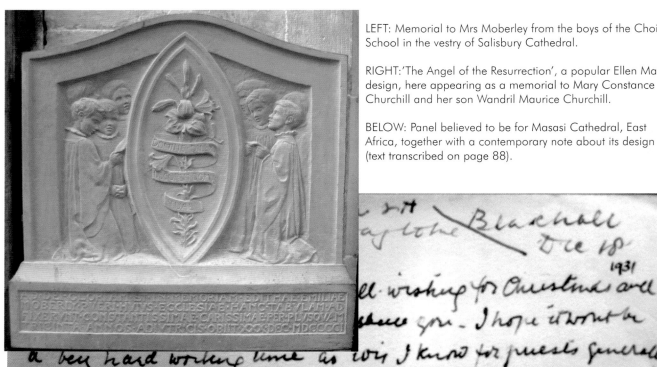

LEFT: Memorial to Mrs Moberley from the boys of the Choir School in the vestry of Salisbury Cathedral.

RIGHT: 'The Angel of the Resurrection', a popular Ellen Mary design, here appearing as a memorial to Mary Constance Churchill and her son Wandril Maurice Churchill.

BELOW: Panel believed to be for Masasi Cathedral, East Africa, together with a contemporary note about its design (text transcribed on page 88).

Merton Church, Norfolk

BELOW: Stone House School, Broadstairs, war memorial, (now relocated).

Following the Dolphin Signed. Plaster Cast 58' x 10' Private Collection

JOG ON JOG ON THE FOOTPATH WAY AND MERRILIE HENT THE STILE A MERRIE HEART GOES ALL THE WAY YOUR SAD TIRES IN A MILE A.
Plaster Cast 1896 Signed 48' x 10' Private Collection

Following the flying fish. Plaster Cast 1905 Signed 58' x 10' Private Collection

LEFT: Two sets of nativity figures are known to be in existence. One like this contemporary photograph shows, is at Leiston (page 94) and another with an additional kneeling figure is at Blaxhall

Probably the companion piece to the bronze opposite.

Hagar and Ishmael

This bronze was purchased through the Felix Cobbold Bequest for the Ipswich Museums Collection. Titled 'No. 276 Miss EM Rope Price £20 - Companion to 272'. Boys with Palms (bronze) 'Benedictus qui Veniti'.

October 15th 1930
Blaxhall
Near Woodbridge, Suffolk

My dearly beloved nephew

I think you must be back again at Cleobury Mortimer but at any rate this letter will find you. I was very sorry not to be at the cathedral saying the Requiem mass but we only heard of it at the last moment and had made our arrangements before coming up. Ned, Kit and I went to St Paul's and Dorothy and Tor went to the Requiem, all meeting afterwards at Deodar Road and staying the night. It was a beautiful service at St Paul's but I felt that I would have liked the other and felt it more in real harmony with my thoughts of our Mike. Dear Harry, it must have been a truly terrible ordeal with the deep sorrow in your heart but it was a great honour too from every point of view and you must have needed divine help to carry it through. I needn't tell you how greatly we all feel this irreparable loss and the strange and terrible manner of it but your mother's letter and Benjy's were so ardently brave and high hearted that they have helped us I think to look at it in the best way. You have no doubt read the paragraph on page 8 of The Times for October 10th on the men of R101 which gives a fine idea of the single-hearted aim of Mike and his co-workers. He always seemed to me almost more than human in his gentle strength. On Sunday at Blaxhall when kneeling at the altar I looked up at the Archangel Michael in the window and a white light coming on it from outside made it seem to change and almost speak to me. It will henceforth be a memorial for both our Michaels, little Arthur Michael in whose memory it was placed there and our Mike whose portrait it undoubtedly was 'the perfect knight'. Ned sends his love very much. It is to him of course a greater personal loss even than to us for they were much like father and son in some ways. Anyway, Mike never spared any trouble or pains or length of journey when he could do anything for Ned and Ned looked upon him as well nigh infallible.

What a great honour it was to take a service at that beautiful cathedral with the Cardinal present I suppose. There were snapshots of you in some of the papers as no doubt you know.

With love and sympathy from us all with you all,

Your affectionate aunt, NELL

Letter by Ellen Mary Rope to her nephew H.E.G.Rope

Some of the details in the East window at Blaxhall Church are as below:

The Incarnation The Word was made Flesh
The Blessed Virgin with Holy Child in centre panel
Lillies and roses are blooming beside him behind is seen the cattle shed with the ox and ass and the manger. On the roof of the shed is the Holy Dove, at the mother's feet a lamb. The dark arms of the cross are dimly seem above, upheld by Angels. Underneath St.Joseph works at his calling to maintain the family, an Angel watches him from the doorway.

St.Peter as patron Saint (in the panel on the right) wearing red (the color of love) his fishers net is over his shoulder, his key in his hand, at his feet grow samphire.

St.John the Evangelist (in opposite panel) an eagle on his right and on his shoulder rest[s] the Dove. Centre light in memory of the Ropes father and mother. Background is that of the neighbourhood. The Mill is there to keep in mind Blaxhall Mill. The Vine appropriate to Blaxhall, where one of the first vines was planted in England about 1532. St.Stephen in memory of the brother Stephen who died young and St.Luke in memory of the brother who was a doctor. St.Stephen is represented kneeling hold a stone in his hand. St.Luke is seated with a book in his hand.

LEFT: Letter from Ellen Mary to her nephew Harry Rope about the tragic death of his brother, her nephew, Michael Rope, in the R101 airship disaster. She refers to the East window in Blaxhall Church, OPPOSITE, made by her niece Margaret Rope, Michael's sister, who used him as the model for St. Michael the archangel, bottom right of the window (in armour).

ABOVE: Description of the same window on the reverse of an Ada Mannall photograph of the window (see page 16) in her handwriting and also transcribed above. The reference to the boy who died young should be Arthur (see page 94).

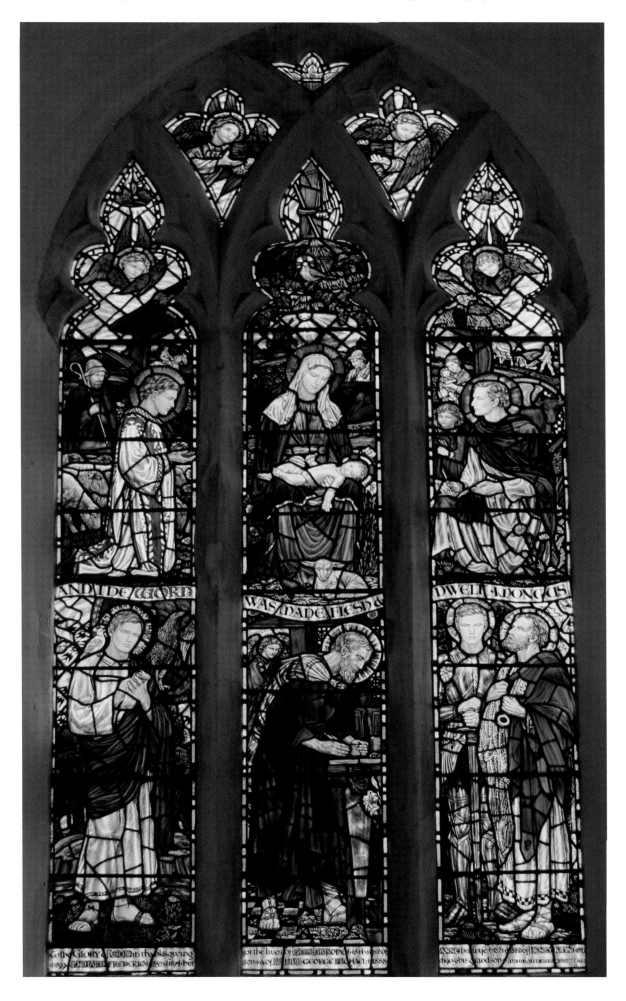

DECK THOU MY HEART O GOD
THAT IT MAY PROVE
A BETTER LODGING THAN A RACK OR GRAVE

One of the ideals of the artists of the Arts and Crafts Movement was to apply their designs to everyday objects and make them affordable to people of 'relatively modest means' (see page 79). Here are some examples by Ellen Mary, including the use of various media (opposite centre and bottom).

Ellen Mary Rope exhibits at the Royal Academy[1]

1885	David playing before Saul	Low relief
	Children in apple tree	Low relief
	Cupid shooting	Low relief
1886	The parting of Hector and Andromache	Relief
1889	Hagar and Ishmael	Relief
	Demeter and Persephone	Relief
	Children playing	Plaque
	Children piping	Plaque
1890	Design of children for a mantelpiece (2)	Relief
	Portrait	Medallion
	Boy on Dolphin	Medallion
	The four elements – earth, air, fire and water	Bas relief
1891	Zephyrus	Bronze relief
1893	Mother and child	Bronze relief
	Music	Relief
	Sculpture	Relief
1895	Guardian angel	Relief
1897	Children bringing lilies to the Holy Child	Relief
	A guardian angel	Bronze relief
	A dream of the sea	Relief
1898	The kingdom of the child	Medallion
	A sea chariot	Bronze medallion
	Antic sport and blue-eyed pleasures frisking light in frolic measures	Low relief
1899	Roland, Margery, Nigel and Rosalind	Bronze relief
1903	Panel for organ chamber	Low relief
1904	Design for electric bell-push	Relief
1905	Caritas	Relief
	A race through the surf	Relief
1907	A bell-ringer	Bronze relief
1908	Will o' the wisp	Relief
	Life's golden age	Relief
1909	Springtime	Relief
1910	Salve	Decorative panel
	St Cecilia	Memorial relief

Demeter and Persephone, exhibited 1889

	Incarnatus est	Memorial relief
1911	The coming of peace	Relief
1912	Charity	Relief
1914	The annunciation	Panels
1917	Pax mundi	Plaque
	St George	Bronze memorial plaque
1918	Even there also thy right hand shall lead me	Memorial relief

[1] Graves 1970(a) for data from 1905 onwards
Graves 1970(b) for data to 1904

CHAPTER FOUR

Ginny Sullivan

HEROES AND UNSUNG HEROES

Introduction

In the spring of 1974 a young PhD student from Leeds arrived in Snape. Ginette Dunn (now Ginny Sullivan) was making her first field-trip to this corner of Suffolk to begin her studies into the popular singing traditions of East Suffolk. Her study area was the two villages of Snape and Blaxhall and her objective was to try and describe a small community through its singing. Ginette explains that her main concern was to present an account that was 'of its moment' and was contextual and descriptive, rather than time-worn, textual and prescriptive. She needed to describe the historical background and social setting of the communities in order to give them their own context, both in time as well as spatially, and to understand the aesthetics of the singing tradition and its significance within the communities The performances needed to be regarded in context, where the singing events and practices, and the singers and their audiences, provide a model for local life and values, and they live out these values in their singing activities. Central to the tradition is the pub, where most of the singing occurs, and surrounding this village environment are alternative places for other types of performance. Within this network the dynamic of the tradition exists.

Her *modus operandii* for this research was, principally, using oral testimony, which meant that her main field method was that of tape-recording long conversations with the villagers in question. She began fieldwork in April 1974, and continued until late 1976. During this time, she was based at the Institute of Dialect and Folk Life Studies at the University of Leeds, and travelled to Suffolk as often as possible for stays of a week or two weeks at a time. During these visits she recorded villagers who quickly became friends and then went with them to their pubs, socials and clubs. She recorded 200 hours of tape on a Uher Report 2000 L reel-to-reel machine. In all, she recorded 20 major singing evenings and a total of 350 different songs; the bulk of the other tapes were made in the homes of individuals.

As Ginette states, her fieldwork method was mainly as a participating observer, with camera and tape-recorder carefully framing her questions and recording songs that were freely given or requested by her. The outcome of her work was a doctoral thesis entitled 'Popular Singing Traditions in and around Snape and Blaxhall' completed in the Institute of Dialect and Folk Life Studies, University of Leeds, 1977. However, the story doesn't end there. As there was sufficient data available from her research and the subject was of popular interest, she re-visited the subject and published a book in 1980 called *The Fellowship of Song – Popular Singing Traditions in East Suffolk.* Now sadly out of print (but maybe something this archive group could resurrect), the book is still sought after by folk music aficionados.

Ginette's recordings lay in the Leeds University vaults for three decades, the closure of the Institute of Dialect and Folk Studies in 1983 meaning that the archives became somewhat neglected. The bulk of the archives was moved to the Special Collections of the Brotherton Library in the early 1990s but

Ginny Sullivan

'Central to the tradition is the pub, where most of the singing occurs...' Blaxhall Ship circa 1953

remained relatively inaccessible as there was no comprehensive funding aid for their contents. The unfulfilled potential of this valuable cultural resource was finally recognised by Drs Clive Upton and Oliver Pickering, who collectively forwarded a bid to the Arts and Humanities Research Board's Resource Enhancement Scheme for funding for a project that would again make them accessible to researchers and would also ensure their long-term preservation. The archive was renamed the Leeds Archive of Vernacular Culture and a major three-year project began in 2002 to arrange a searchable catalogue and to digitise the extensive collection of sound recordings. They are now available for such a community-based project as this book.

They are a primary resource that has remained untapped except for Ginette's own research. Some of the characters included in this chapter have slipped into village mythology: Priscilla Savage, for example, immortalised in George Ewart Evans' *Ask the Fellows Who Cut the Hay*, whilst Alf 'Wicketts' Richardson and Cyril Poacher can be seen, with many others, in the Kennedy/Lomax film 'Here's To The Health of The Barley Mow' and then, later, on tape cassette and CD recordings of them singing their songs. So we have seen and heard a number of them - icons of Blaxhall's past - but through Ginette's work we have a new angle to approach them, for these are their own words illustrating their thoughts, their beliefs and their aspirations. It is as near as 'from the horses

mouth' as you can get. These transcripts are not totally verbatim - we have deleted the repeated sentences for ease of reading; also, we have removed the 'ehs, arghs' and 'pardons'! Some of these villagers were old and undoubtedly hard of hearing and Ginette's New Zealand accent was a challenge to some, as was, probably, their Suffolk was to her.

The recordings are of various lengths, as some interviewees were probably more forthcoming than others, but taken together the recollections contain within them an interesting insight into village life of the Suffolk Sandlings during the first seven decades of the 20th century.

Ginny Sullivan

Fieldwork in the Crown at Snape. Ginette, Bob Hart, Percy Webb and others.

Ginny Sullivan

Alice Maud Messenger neé Ling

Born 1905 known as 'Maudie' Ling. Her father was Esau Ling and her mother came from Cambridge. In service until her marriage in 1934 to Chris Messenger.

Recorded in Aldeburgh 4 October 1974.
We used to have Church socials and little concert parties and go to other villages. It was organised by our Church choir mistress, no payment – all for free and a cup of tea. I was up at the school when I was two weeks over two years old then when I was three I was on the stage and scared stiff!

During the first war we used to have concerts and I would sing and I used to sing in the church choir. We used to make up our own things for the church choir, we would choose a popular song of the day and then get the youngsters to act it. Us older ones would dress up and act the parts. We had a church choir and we had an organist who was very good, I learnt a lot of songs from her. We would go to Ipswich and round Woolworth's and get sixpence sheets of music. Our organist was good and when you were with her you had to sing properly which probably helped me to learn how to sing correctly. There is a certain way to sing, keeping in time with the music, and noticing all the stops, and to sing clearly. We had a schoolmaster at school who took a great interest in singing and he made sure the words sounded distinctive so the listener could understand what you were singing about. What I liked about the old songs is that they have got a

story behind them. Some of these singers today, you don't know what they are singing about.

Another thing they used to do – if you go round the corner I used to live there in the first house, anyway there used to be a three-cornered green there and the women would dance on there. Dance over the lighted candle and I have seen them doing that. I remember I was a kid on holiday, I think it was Whit Monday. It took some doing you know because they had long skirts and you would see them pick their dresses up and dance over the lighted candle. They weren't to put it out. Bessie was a dab hand at that. I can't remember mother doing it, I know Aunt Anne did it and I've see her and Aunt Emma do it. I was only a kiddie and I wasn't suppose to be looking at them. They would take it right serious. Only the women and not the men, it was nothing to do with them.

A lot of the old Blaxhall types originated from gypsies – right far back. They used to be here the Romanies, that's their proper name. They were here on the Common, really before the first war. After that they started drifting away. And there all gone now.

By adding tarmac to the road the 'three cornered green' had become much smaller. By 2009 no green remains.

My father [Esau Ling] was a smallholder or market gardner and lived down by the Ship, near where the little shop is – it was a house on that side. He grew vegetables, a little barley and a little oats, then potatoes, carrots all on about five or six acres. He rented it from the estate, the Ullswater Estate. In those days Lord Ullswater, he was speaker of the House of Commons, he had much of the land around here. My mother and father met in London where my father worked. My mother's maiden name was Bye and she came from Cambridge. My grandfather also worked the smallholding and he died and my grandmother encouraged my father to come back to Blaxhall to work their land. Otherwise, I wouldn't be here as I was born in London and I would probably still be in London.

Stone picking with my father; dropping potatoes, picking beans, picking peas, picking up potatoes, picking up acorns, picking blackberries there was always something to be done. Chopping up the food to give to the horses. Then there was going to the farms for the milk in the mornings, we would have to walk down to Dunningworth Hall for the milk. First to the Fir Tree Farm then Dunningworth

Esau Ling (left), Ben Ling (centre) and David 'Nipper' Ling on their smallholding.

then home for breakfast. Then we would walk to Wickham Market for people's medicine then return – that was ten miles and we got threepence for that.

I didn't sing in the Ship but when my uncles and aunts would come down of a weekend, they would sing in the house after leaving the Ship and as a child I would be listening from my bedroom and that's how I learnt some of my songs.

Ginny Sullivan

Dunningworth Hall circa 1974

When I left school I went into service. A lady came to see my mother and she said, 'You have a girl leaving school, can I have her?' And there wasn't any question about it, you had to go where you told. My first job was housework at Red House Farm for two shillings and sixpence a week plus your keep, of course, and half a day a week and every other Sunday off. And the Sunday you didn't come out, you had to go to church in the morning. Then I went to Cambridge and I went to work for one of my uncles who kept a shop, and do the housework as his wife was an invalid. Mind you I was only 14 when I went there and I left there when I was 18 and come home for a few weeks then off I went to London. I was in London two years then I went to Manchester and I was up there seven years then I came home and went to Halesworth then I came to Blaxhall after all that wandering.

And that was 40 years ago as I have been married 40 years. There were all housework jobs where I was the only person, so I had to do everything. If I could have my time again I would have preferred to go where there were two or three staff, it would have made things easier. Though I always wanted to be a barmaid, though I don't know that I ever got the chance - as a girl always had to go into service. That was hard, up at six and to bed by 11pm – it was hard work.

When I got married it was hard times then, which I wouldn't like to see again. My husband worked down Snape Maltings for 28 shillings a week which was only seasonal, usually until 1st June then he had to try and find some other work of which there was very little. Then the war came and there was plenty of work on the 'dromes for those left behind. What a time though – air raids – doodlebugs. There was a battle school here, I remember tanks used to be outside our house and they would go round and round and round and the cups in the pantry used to jabber and cracks came in the walls. But it was the doodlebugs I didn't like. Still we got through that.

Mrs Fletcher played the piano and she was the church organist and she gave music lessons too. My daughter went to her for a little while and she past two exams. She would play the piano at our concerts. I could sing better with her playing the piano. She had several go down to her to learn music.

When I left school in 1919 there were 101 or 102 at school and then that gradually went down. They were big families in those days and now I suppose there are 250 to 300 in the village. Tunstall and Blaxhall men never could agree same with

Snape people when I was little. They seemed to be foreigners as we didn't know them and we were in our own little world here. But then things improved at the First World War with people getting about more especially if you could get a bike. Before the 14 War there weren't many bikes about but by the war there were more about and if you could get one you were well away. But that was the start of it – chaps broke out and got with others.

Picking blackberries, an annual Blaxhall event , they either went for jam or for dyeing - maybe Alice is in the Ada Mannall photograph

Known Repertoire - recorded and unrecorded ALICE MESSENGER

Recorded	Title	Recording
	Are We to Part Like This?	
	Beautiful Dreamer	
	Cockles and Mussels	
	Count Your Blessings	
	English Rose	
	For Old Time's Sake	
	Gypsy's Warning	
	I Passed by Your Window	
	I Will Take You Home Again, Kathleen	
	If I Could Plant a Seed of Love	
	If Those Lips Could Only Speak	
	In the Shade of the Old Apple Tree	
	It's a Great Big Shame	
	Just an Old Fashioned Lady	
	Just Like Ivy	
	Lassie from Lancashire	
	London is the Largest City in the World	
	Meet Me Tonight in Dreamland	
	My Grandfather's Clock	
	Nelly Dean	
	Old Rustic Bridge	
	Poor Old Joe	
	Smiling Through	
	Sweet Rosie O'Grady	
	Two Little Girls in Blue	
	Volunteer Organist	
	When the Fields are White with daisies	
	Where the Praeties Grow	
	White Wings	
	Won't You Buy My Pretty Flowers?	

Data : Ginette Dunn, 1980; Keith Summers, 1998

Ben Ling

Born 1891 to Laura Ling, who had been in service in London. Brought up by grandparents and uncle in Blaxhall. Attended school and evening classes. Emigrated to Canada and farmed there. Returned to serve in the First World War. Undertook various work. Married Eva Andrews, had two sons.

Recorded in Blaxhall 2 July 1975

I began to sing a long time ago when I was very young and used to go to different places, you know, like Iken and Woodbridge. I went mostly with the British Legion when we had a branch here [in Blaxhall]. I sung at the Ship once, when some people down from London to give a prize – that's a long time ago you know – they gave a prize for first, second and third and I won the first prize.

I learnt myself to sing – it was a gift I never had no training. I might have done as I used to drive some people to Woodbridge for Mr Rope and they went to singing lessons as he wanted me to go in and join them but I wouldn't, I used to drive them up there and wait until they come out. Otherwise I might have had lessons like Frank Reeve, he went you see. It was mostly for the choir for Blaxhall Church that went, it was really done to train the voices but I never went so I trained my own. I'm getting on now, getting past singing – I'm 84. I can't give it as much force as I used to 'cos time won't allow for it. I can hum one out half decent but not like I used to.

We used to have a club up here at Blaxhall and we would have a dinner then we would sing up there. Several of us would sing there. I sang as a boy and when I went to school the teacher told me I had a good voice then when I was about 17 I went to Canada and then the war came on and I came back then - three years and a half out in France and I used to sing out there and the forces used to come and listen in a dugout when things went quiet we used to get to singing – it used to amuse the officers – it was a way to cheer ourselves up. We used to sit in a dugout five or six of us and when it was a bit quiet. I was in the 'tillary in the war, Field Artillary. I paid my fare from Canada back home, I wanted to join the 'tillary in Canada but there wasn't no room so I come home.

I was born in London and came down here and lived with my grandparents and that is where I've been ever since except I went away to Canada then the Army, so I was brought up here. Started farming, my uncle and me, on a field but we never done very well off it. Dry weather and things. That was in 1919 when things were very slack.

When I went to Canada I had two good jobs out there on a farm. Very nice people I got on well out there. I worked for Ebna Corby they had two farms, two little farms, they were Scotch. He, Ebna

Ginny Sullivan

Ben Ling and his wife Eva, Blaxhall, June 1975

Corby, had a wife, and children, and his sister and his mother all there in the farmhouse. And we got on well there, we used to get to singing of a night time, had a schoolteacher playing the piano and a singing at night in the winter time as you couldn't do much.

My grandparents who lived in Blaxhall were Lings, David Ling was my grandfather. This place was full of Lings one time more than what is now. My uncle's name in Blaxhall was Elisha.

When I came back to Blaxhall after the war I worked in the railways and then they amalgamated the railways together and I got stood off like a lot more did. So then we hired this land, down where you go to Snape we had a field which is planted with trees now. Me and my uncle we sort of farmed that for several years we had an old Ford van and used to go back and forwards to Aldeburgh with vegetables and fruit and we drove that for several years. I drove that old Ford for 13 years and it never went into a garage only once. Then I left that and went to Wantisden where they had built a camp for miners from Durham, all unemployed and they come down and we built that camp. Then I worked there for six months used to help put the huts up but there all gone now. There was a lot built there, I got on alright there.

Then I went from there to work on the Lowther 'state [Estate] in the Forest timber. I was only there for a season. Then I went in the Council I was there 20 years then I retired from there when I was 65 then I have been knocking about on me own since to earn a shilling.

My parents lived in London, my father was a Londoner but my mother was born in Blaxhall and moved to London as a young girl as a lot did go up there. Mostly the songs I learnt was when I was in London, we used to go to the theatre and hear a song and I could practically learn it if I heard it once. That's where I picked a lot of them up. Used to go to the Hippodrome at Ipswich when I lodged at Ipswich when I was on the railways.

I was about 12 [1903] when I first would go to the Ship where the old boys would sing the old songs. You could go in there but you weren't allowed to drink, the landlords were strict. So we used to get behind the high settles like Aaron Ling and 'Croney' his brother they used to get in there singing in the Ship, all the old fashioned songs. I believe Cyril Poacher used to learn his songs off his grandfather that was his grandfather what we called 'Croney'.

I've been to the Snape 'Plough' and the 'Key' at Snape and sang. We used to have an outing of

had to leave off being in Blaxhall, so nobody sleep there now. Well, there isn't any travellers now, is there? We don't call them gypsies we call them travelling people now.

Now Mrs Bailey, she's still alive. She was a real towering woman, ever so clean. Her name was Smith, really she came from Lowestoft. She used to have a lovely white apron and she was worth looking at when she came to the door. She didn't press you to buy anything, she would say, 'Is there anything you need today?' That's all she would say. Her daughter, Lizzie married Horrie Bennett and they lived there on Tunstall Common. They used to sell laces and buttons and tape both white and black, all that sort of thing. And a quarter of tea, always a quarter of tea you could buy off them.

Blaxhall isn't like it used to be, people don't cling together, they ain't got no love for one another. Years ago if you were ill or they were ill your neighbour come in and do a day's work for you; do your washing for you, but they don't do that now, you have to send it to the laundry and pay for it yourself. Everything is so different today.

Pork in the pot – We used to have what we called brine. We had saltpetre and salt and we used to rub the pork in pieces and put them in the pot until it was full. Then if you wanted a piece you would take it out and boil it. Though we don't have to do it ourselves now, well they won't let you kill a pig without a licence, do they? We used to kill a pig, sell half and keep half and then put half of it in the pot and then we always had a bit of meat in the house so we didn't need to buy it like we do now. Mrs Reeve got me a piece the other day and that was one pound six for a bit of bacon. That's a nice piece but that's a lot of money.

Extracts from 15 November 1974
My husband – being a shepherd he used to go away of a morning at 7 o'clock and didn't come home until 7 o'clock at night. And he used to sit up with the sheep all night when they were lambing and then he would come home and have his breakfast then go again. If there was a mother what had some babies and wont mother them he would take them to a hut where he had a straw bed and he used to put them in there. And there was a fire on the stove, where he used to heat the milk to give to the lambs so they had warm milk. And then when there was a mother that had dead lambs he would take the coat off the dead one and put it on a live one and then run it with that mother. She would take it like that but not without.

He had just 200 sheep while the shepherd up here [Lime Tree] had 500, a big flock but 200 was what they had at Grove Farm. That was who my husband was shepherd for – Mr Rope. But when the lambs were big enough and they went together he would go from Blaxhall up unto the heath and they used to feed up there and then at dinner time he would come home and I used to meet him at the bottom of this hill here and take his bag and take his coat. He would put his sheep in his fold then he would come home and have his meal. Then in the afternoon he would go and set the hurdles all round, so one fold would be ready for tomorrow, so you always had one fold for your sheep to go into. The turnips they used to live on and some sort of meal they used to give them, and they had that in a trough and the sheep would go along there and feed. A shepherd's life was a very interesting life if anybody liked shepherding.

Now when I had him small (Will) I used to go and sit up with dad, I would lay him on the bed and would sit up with him. I didn't like to be at home alone. When we first married his father used to sit up with him 'cos he wont more than 24 and I wont more than 22 so we weren't very old people and you didn't want to sleep alone at night. And where the sheep yard used to be – down here below right by the road and you didn't know who might walk onto you.

And he went from here after Mr Rope sold the sheep, he went to Blaxhall Hall. Mr Thompson used to be shepherd and he died and dad Bob took his place. And then of course he had to walk there evening and morning. And they would take some sheep away and they would go as far as Parham and then he would have to walk home and many nights he wont home until 7 o'clock. Shepherding was a life of very hard work. He would take the hurdles – one in front on a stick and five behind and he would carry them and set those hurdles for next day's food.

He started down at Mr Rope's as a backh'us boy and then you see my uncle [Robert Russell] used to be shepherd, well, he was going to age and he give up shepherding and Mr Rope asked when my husband was eighteen [1889], he asked him would he take the shepherd's job, and 'cos he took it. We don't have a flock of sheep around here at all now. The nearest flock is Sir Peter Greenwell at Butley Abbey. But there's none round here, nor Farnham or Glemham or Tunstall none at all.

Preacher comes to Blaxhall - Priscilla back row second from the left (holding child)

Harvest Supper in the Ship before 1911 – They used to hire the Big Room for the harvest Supper. The mother's of the men they used to cook the meat and the vegetables and they would have a dinner there. And the children would all go to a house on the corner here by the green with a lady who would look after them. And we would play games like ludo and snakes and ladders. And the man at the Ship would heat a frying pan and put in some halfpennies and he would make them hot and then from the window he throw them out and we used to scramble for them – what we called 'hot halfpennies'.

They would hire the Big Room, and one woman would boil the beef, one the carrots and so on and we had batter puddings with it. And I was a baby and that used to be an old-fashioned way of having a Harvest Supper. But that isn't the same now.

Preaching – A gentleman, Mr Finbow from Framlingham, used to give an open air service on the common here. He would give a chapel service as an open-air meeting. He would stand out on that green down here and Mr Bridges would bring a piano and his wife used to play the hymns and you would get a real lot of men sitting alongside the green. The men that didn't go to church would get there to hear him preach, he would come to Snape chapel to preach sometimes.

Extracts from 11 September 1974
I love children, I had 12 myself and I brought up eight of them. I had one, dear boy, drowned at Iken Cliff, he was 17 year old, he'd be a man bigger than Willie now. He'd been working in the morning, and he had had a good dinner and of course he couldn't swim and he got in one of those pools what draw you. He didn't come up until the second day, that's why I don't like Iken Cliff. You used to go there when the children were small. You would pack up a dinner bag and take them there and have a picnic at Iken Cliff. And the children used to think as much of that as if they had gone to the seaside. We used to go up on the heath up here, used to have a picnic up there but they say that it is so grown up you can't get up there. But I think the soldiers had part of it to practice but they say it is all too tall to get up there now. I haven't been up there for over a year, we used to go there for a walk. Trouble is I get so tired. They say,'You should have a walking stick', but I said' I'm too proud to have a walking stick!'

Rabbit Pie – Skin the rabbit, wash, cut it in the joints and have the legs and the shoulders and the back but the head and the neck you use to boil them and that would be be the gravy and then you could put that in your pie dish. I've got two pie dishes now that I had when I was first married. A chicken pie dish and a rabbit pie dish. We didn't buy the meat

Priscilla (left) when she was in service

But they don't make them now – they don't get the rabbits.

There used to be a man at Friston of the name of Blake. Him and his brother used to hire the rabbitting up here and they used to go all round the hedges and get the rabbits and sell them. But they don't do that now, they poison them now and they get that myxomatosis so that people are afraid to eat a rabbit.

Lenny, last week, ran over one and killed it and he took it home and flayed it and Violet made a rabbit pie and he said, 'It made you think of old times'.

I was abed one time, not very well, and my Percy was making and the doctor come and he said, 'What you got in there, boy?'. And he said, 'I'm making some soup for the boy's dinner.' So he said,'What you got in there?'. And Percy said, 'Two sparrows, yes, and I've got some onions, carrots and turnips – and I've got some swimmers' – that was dumplings. And the doctor said, 'Give us a cup, boy'. So he gave the poor old boy a cup of soup which he drank saying, 'Their take no harm at that'. That's all that was in it, just two sparrows, they used have bricks, one on the other and bring one down and that would kill the sparrow. They had a trail of corn under the brick and the one at that end used to have a bit of string on. They would pull it and it would land on the sparrow and kill it. That's how they got their living but they don't do that now.

like they do now. Then you lay your rabbit in and a piece or two of fattening pork. Some people have the real fat pork, and then you put a crust on the top, put the gravy in first then put the crust on the top then bake it. You would have to give it two hours to bake itself properly and then that used to be your Sunday morning breakfast. That was a regular thing to have rabbit pie Sunday morning.

Under the oak behind Ivydene - Left to right: Violet, Len, Priscilla, David, George, Evie and Daphne.

Ginny Sullivan

Two icons of Blaxhall past - Priscilla Savage and Alf 'Wicketts' Richardson out side Ivydene c. 1970s.

Known Repertoire - recorded and unrecorded PRISCILLA SAVAGE

Recorded	*Title*	*Recording*
	Grief, O Grief	
	If I Were a Blackbird	
	Johnson (Two Jolly Sportsmen)	
	William, Dearest William	

Data : Ginette Dunn, 1980; Keith Summers, 1998

Bessie Hammond neé Howell

Born c.1896 in Staffordshire then moved to Yorkshire was the daughter of a miner. Went to Blackpool in service, worked there as a nurse during the First World War. Met her future husband there, Henry Hammond, married him in 1920 and moved to Blaxhall. He was a horseman for Grove Farm. He died after only nine years of marriage. Bess did housework and nursing, raised two daughters alone. Moved from Blaxhall in 1976 to a pensioner's cottage in Woodbridge.

Recorded at home in Blaxhall - 2 October 1974

My husband's name was Henry Hammond and he used to live in the Old Barn Cottages and he was horseman for Mr Teddy Rope down at Grove, that was before he went in the Forces. Then when he came back [from the war] he went back to it for a little while but he couldn't work long because he had got TB. We hadn't been married long about nine years, we married when he was 24 and he was gone by the time he was 33. And he was in the Sanatorium at Ipswich, Foxhall Road nearly half the time. He went out to Russia after the Armistice had been signed and they say he got it out there but it didn't show itself until later.

I would pick up my songs off the wireless. I would work at the canning factory at Woodbridge - in the summer time they would have fruit; strawberries and plums and in the winter time; carrots and potatoes and peas. And I would always be singing – they said 'you know when Bess is here she has singing on the brain'. When we used to go in the canteen at Woodbridge in the dinner hour we used to sing there.

I remember Bessie Ling, she had an accordion and she would step-dance as well. She was a rare lively

woman, a real country woman. I had never been in a pub in my life until I came here. How I came to go this Blaxhall Ship was during the wartime, they used to send their children down to the country and I would have them. Well, it came that the mothers and fathers would come too. Then they would come for holidays as they liked it so much, and they would go to the pub. They said, 'Are you coming for a drink?'. And I said 'I've never been in a pub in my life', but I went along. Then some said they had heard me singing at home and would I sing a few songs. So then one thing led to another, like it does.

I was born in Staffordshire then my parents moved to Pontefract, Yorkshire when I was six months old. My father had come to Yorkshire to work in the pits. My maiden name was Howell.

I was in service in Blackpool and I said one day, 'Come on let's join up and do our bit'. So we went along to the recruiting office and we had to go through all the rigmarole like soldiers and the marching and the drilling and all. So we were all in service so we all gave our notice in and joined up. And I worked in a hospital looking after wounded soldiers. And my future husband was there in the medical corps. And we got to walking out together and there was the Armistice and he got called away to Russia. and I didn't hear from him for some time, it was ages and ages. And I thought that's it then. But he did come back and he looked me up and we got married.

Working in service in those days was not made easy for you. We had a lot of scrubbing and cleaning these big old-fashioned stoves and a lot of steelwork. I was a woman of all trades, done a bit of everything. When I put my girls to service, Pat was a parlour maid, the youngest and the eldest one went to another big house and she was like me and did a bit of everything, that one. There was nothing else to do then but to go into service but they won't do that today, will they? Won't go into that sort of thing today. Well theres more factories about now [to work in]. In those day the lad's went in the pits and the girls into service.

After the game there would be a Quoits Supper for the men. My husband was a quoits player and at the end of the season we would have a supper. Mrs Savage would cook the potatoes and someone else would cook the meat. Then two or

three women would come up and lay the tables and wash up and that's when I sang my first song here in Blaxhall parish rooms that's 50 years ago [1924]. And I think it was Prissie Savage that said, 'Come on Bessie, you can give us a song'. And my husband watched me with surprise as I got up and sang a song. We went home in silence that night and I thought, Oh dear I've done it now. But we got home and made a cup of tea then he said 'Thanks for making the dinner and the singing. I never knew you could sing like that!'. And that was the very first song I sang here.

When I first went to the Blind [RNIB] there was a lady there who might come round, she came to entertain us and she would play the piano and of course you had to join in the songs. So we did join in and she heard me singing and she said,'Whose that singing? Someone's singing in here that's got a bit of talent'. So they said, 'Well its Mrs Hammond. So she came to me and said, 'Who taught you to sing?' I said, 'Nobody, I just pick 'em up'. She said, 'Do you know if you had had training when you were younger you could have been a good singer'. Because she said, 'it's in you'.

Blaxhall WI Christmas Party - Bessie Hammond is furthest right

Known Repertoire - recorded and unrecorded BESSIE HAMMOND

Recorded   *Title*   *Recording*

Broken Doll
Don't Go Down in the Mine, Dad
If I had My Way
If You Ever Go Across the Sea to Ireland
If Those Lips Could Only Speak
In the Heart of Lancashire
My Souvenirs
Springtime in the Rockies
Tours Till the Stars Lose Their Glory

Data : Ginette Dunn, 1980; Keith Summers, 1998

Lenny Savage

Born 1913, son of Priscilla and Robert Savage. Various early jobs then went with the County Council from 1929. In the Army during the Second World War, moved from Blaxhall to Snape after his return. Married with one son and one daughter.

Recorded at home in Snape 18 July 1974

Blaxhall was where I was bred and born, my father was a shepherd, he was on Grove Farm, where I started as a backh'us boy. In fact I used to go there before I left school, I would go there Saturdays and work in the garden. Then I went as backh'us boy for about a year, I suppose. That's when I first left school then I went down here and worked on a rabbit farm and that was when I first started doing rabbits, really.

Then I went away on the old steam engines as cook boy with my brother and I had a year with Dawsons then I come on the Council and I've been on the Council ever since. So I've been with these old engines and things since 1929 until steam went out.

Down at the Ship in the old days, nearly everybody used to sing and the custom was that the one who sung the song could call on the next and that's how they usually went round – sing, say or pay. Then they would mix it up with a bit of step-dancing but now that's all gone, the step-dancers have all gone. They don't have the booze ups and the women dancers aren't there. You see all the women used to step dance. Dance in pairs, fours and singles, always accompanied by one button accordion down at the Ship.

They would sing all their own songs but most of the women singers, them old girls, have gone now. Percy Ling's wife, well, she was a beautiful singer. That was a few years ago, and she would play accordion and sing. She'd be a star turn on her own. Their family, they all used to play in that family.

Yes, I knew old Brightwell and his sons, old Brightwell he was over ninety when he was still singing. And I suppose his sons will be seventy odd now. They used to call him 'Velvet' on account that he wore a velvet jacket, I've got one upstairs.

We used to play quoits, steel quoits, well that was a sure reason for a sing song. There were no such things as licences, you just got a barrel of beer from the pub and humped it up there and just sold it. Probably put a copper or two on it, for the trouble and that was that. Mind you, somebody had to bring some jars and somebody had to pay for the lot of it. A shilling a bottle all round, darks and light and that sort of thing. They still do at the Flower Shows now, on the quiet. We used to have two quoits teams, a first and a second team at Blaxhall. Nearly every village had a quoits team and Saturdays, was competition night. They used to play in a league for a cup standing about this high. But there's not above three quoits beds now,

Messrs Dawsons of Rushmere, Ipswich, Suffolk - Threshing at Butley. Percy Savage is the young man, third from left, Lenny was cookboy.

there's one at Woodbridge at Warwick Road, one at Ipswich at the Rosary and Butley is the other one.

And another thing they had was bell-ringers, Blaxhall had a wonderful set of bells, they got six bells there. There was a father and three sons rung all of them, one or two came from outside. Well Monday night was always bell-ringing night, always bell-ringing practice Monday night. They would ring until about nine, then that lot automatically packed up and go down the Ship. Well, they always finished their ringing over a glass of beer.

Percy Ling, he's a Tunstall Ling, he's not from Blaxhall, that's the difference. They live between Blaxhall and Tunstall, although his not classed as a permanent Blaxhall man, although we went to the same school and the same woodwork centre and that sort of thing. Probably, he spent more time in Blaxhall, more time in the Blaxhall Ship than the Tunstall Green Man.

There's so many Lings in Blaxhall that they had to give them nicknames to define them. So this Ling that I'm referring too, his father was 'Fish' Ling 'cos he went fishing. And they had to define him from

another one that lived down the corner who they called 'Straight' Ling. They called my grandfather just plain Aaron Ling, they called his son, Geoff's father, 'Croppy' Ling that was to define one Ling from the other. Then the other was just Abie Ling, then there was Esau Ling, the fellow that used to take fruit and stuff to Aldeburgh. There was 'Rook' Ling that was my grandfather's cousins, that family were all Lings.

Some such as the Richardsons were relations to the Lings, see you read about the shepherd old Lioney Richardson, well old Lioney and that comes right down the line. Well, a Richardson married a Ling, you see. There was a widow who married a Richardson, then a Ling so she got both.

Extracts recorded at home in Snape 1 October 1974.
I'm going back to the days when there was about four boys and we all would be sitting around the hearth on little stools and that was the days of candles and oil lamps and father would be lambing, sleeping in the hut. So she [Priscilla] would try and sing to us, that was more or less to kill the boredom so we didn't fight or be at one another's throat. Or else there weren't enough light to do anything else. We used to make these old hearth rugs, she would start one herself and we would be working on one

A George Thomas Rope sketch, could this be Robert or his father Tom?

An Ada Mannall photograph of sheep shearing at Grove Farm - is that Robert Savage looking at the camera?

of the corners or cutting the threads ready for her, that sort of thing. Well, we nearly all had a job to do anyway, when that was done. I probably had scrubbed the backh'us, pantry and all that before I was allowed my chance to come and sit near the fire. Clean seven or eight pairs of boots, wash ten or a dozen pairs of stockings – socks. We had to graft, we had to work.

My father couldn't do a sight [much] he was not at home long enough, not with the sheep, many an hour, specially lambing time, which would last six weeks. The oldest one, probably Russell would take his grub back to the fold so he didn't have to come home. Come home once a week for washing and a shave. The lambing fold depended on where they decided to have it that year. They'd run four or five farms together and these flocks would move around the four or five farms where the keep was. Well that was what they usually done was to work their way round and eat the stubbles, until they were ploughed. And they would be working round, so where the root crop and the kale was, would be near the lamb yard. My father had to make his own lamb yard every year with whins. They used to go and cut whins on the heath and put them between two hurdles tied together with broaches. They would stand a row along one way then some the other way[upright] then they would lay some hurdles over the top, probably thatch it with straw or anything and they had a little pen

each sheep to lamb in. Then as they got that they could come away, then they would come out and put them into the fold. They would have a big tilt and run this tilt round to keep the wind from blowing on the little ones when they were small. And they had a forward run, go one ahead all the while, they had a hurdle with a pair of rollers in it so the lambs could squeeze through. They would go through and have an early bite before the mother's did. So they could go backwards and forwards. It was like a weaner hurdle.

Ginette asked what he did in the military. Nine country; Iraq, Iran, Palestine, France, Belgium, Holland, Germany finished up on the Elbe. I didn't get wounded but messed though what caused a lot of this [Lenny's respiratory problems] on the plains of Iraq, dust storms and whatever, you got full of that. I got sand fly fever twice and then they sent us to Palestine. Well that was a damn sight worse 'cos that was humid with the heat there. Got malaria, then we come back for the Second Front, we come back to Jaywick Sands, fancy coming back from Palestine to Jaywick Sands. In chalets on the beach and that was winter time. Well, that was enough to kill any white man. That was a holiday camp, Jaywick Sands, they pushed us in there and we were still training for the Second Front. Where we had to get the vehicles ready and waterproof them to get ready to go back out again.

When I was called up in the ITC [Infantry Training Centre] I went to Portland, right up on the rocks at Portland and it got a bit too warm there for an ITC so they packed it up. It got too hot, we were getting bombed and machine gunned on the square when we were drilling because the Jerries had took the Channel Islands and they were using our 'planes. Just coming over and machine gunning us on the square. That's where our first causalities were, as trainees.

I was there when they were coming back from Dunkirk. Helped to cart some of the soldiers back from Weymouth beach, brought them back into our barracks and they come back and ate all our grub up. Put us on powdered iron rations. Put us under canvas down the moat, then drafted us, split us up into other regiments. I went to the Wiltshire's, the 'Shiny Seventh', at Devizes. Never heard a bomb, never heard a siren there. Before that I was in the Royal Welsh, then the Royal Wilts. And my brother Percy, the one that was at Metfield, he was in the RAFC and he'd got a half tidy number driving ambulances from Scotland down to the hospitals,

MAC. So, then, an older brother could claim a younger brother if he so wished, if he wanted to have him with him. So he said, 'You better come with me, brother'. By the time he claimed me I never did catch up with him. He finished up in Crete and I finished up in Iraq and I never did see him until the war was over.

When I went away I already had two children, Arnold, he was about that height and Daphne, she was a little babe and she was running underneath her [Violet's] skirt when I come home the first time. She didn't know me; she was a babe in arms when I went away. When I came home, he [Arnold] told me to get out of his mother's bed. He went running in the other room saying, 'Mother, there's an old man getting into your bed' – that was his father. That was lovely, after hitch hiking from Devizes, never got home but once a year. When the war was at its worse all leave was cancelled and when we got out to Iraq, well I never got home at all. Not until we came home for the Second Front, we had six weeks furlough then.

Wedding of Lenny and Violet, 20 April 1935 at Iken Church

Known Repertoire - recorded and unrecorded LENNY SAVAGE

Recorded	Title	Recording
	Dark Eyed Sailor	
	Foggy Dew	
	Nancy from Yarmouth	
	Rose of Tralee	
	Volunteer Organist	

Data : Ginette Dunn, 1980; Keith Summers, 1998

Ginny Sullivan

Lily Durrant

Born c. 1914 in Blaxhall. Frank Reeve's sister. Went into service after leaving school at fourteen. Worked in the Women's Land Army during the Second World War, and did other general farm work throughout her life. Her second husband Eli Durrant, died in 1972 aged 58. Had four children.

Recorded at home in Blaxhall 1 July 1975.
Was it your mother who used to sing?- If she'd been here she would have helped you, you know. She used to know some lovely old songs. So did my oldest brother but he's died about two year ago. He used to sing some nice old songs. Her husband used to sing some nice ones, but I don't think she knew them, not properly. I believe she said that she'd got one but she didn't know where to find it what her husband had written out. And it was called, 'Where the Sunset Turns the Ocean Blue to Gold.' That's a lovely song, that was, but I don't expect she know where to lay her hands on it now.

My mother's name was Gertrude Reeve. Reeve by marriage, and Pryke by maiden name. Some of the songs that she used to sing were; 'The Dark-Eyed Sailor', 'If I Were A Blackbird', 'May I Come Home Again', 'Lamplight Down in The Valley'. I know that, my mother used to sing it. Then there was; 'I Wish I Had Someone to Love Me'; 'Someone to Call My Own'. They were very old songs she used to sing. She was eighty-eight when she died. And she'd been in Blaxhall all her life.

She used to sing when she went to weddings and

parties and, you know, they'd get her to sing. She used to sing quite well, used to know them right through you see. I would pick bits up here and there, you know, but not to know them right through. As far as I know my mother didn't sing in the Ship. She could step dance. If she did [sing] that used to be years ago before I come about, before I was born, you know, when they were younger. I think they used to years ago before I was born. She would step-dance at weddings when she used to go to the weddings, you know. My sister's wedding, my brothers' weddings, and she'd dance.

I had three brothers and, three girls. And there's four of us left. Two girls and two boys left. Father was a very quiet man. He got killed, he wasn't very old, well, about sixty-odd. He was very quiet. Oh he'd got in the pub and have a pint of beer and all like that, you know but, in other words he weren't so lively as what we were. He used to do agricultural work. They mostly used to all do that years ago 'cause they didn't have education like they have today. So they used to mostly all do that. The money weren't much either then. Not like it is today. No. But they were happy enough with it anyway. Used to enjoy themself in their little way.

Lily and Eli Durrant step-dancing in The Ship, 1953

	An aged shooting pony	Oil		Anxious mothers	Drawing
	Meadows near Glemham	Oil		Sketch	Drawing
	Evening on the Alde	Oil		Mill on the Chelmer	Drawing
	Meadow scene	Drawing	1900	February	Oil
	Near Dunningworth Hall	Drawing		Nightfall	Oil
1896	An Essex lane	Oil		Spring Afternoon – Blaxhall	Oil
	An old barn at sunset	Oil		Mother and child	Oil
	An Essex homestead	Oil		September	Drawing
	November	Oil		'Out into the night'	Drawing
	Winter evening	Oil		A Night Sketch	Drawing
	Road elms – Essex	Oil		Acorn Time	Drawing
	Attention	Oil		Langham Bridge	Drawing
	Near Kelvedon	Drawing		A Wooden Wall	Drawing
	Layer Breton Mill, Essex	Drawing		Marlesford	Drawing
	Sketch at Hatfield Peverel	Drawing	1901	After the day's rain	Oil
	Foalhood	Drawing		The River Alde at Snape	Oil
	At Hockley, Essex	Drawing		The Alde at Little Glemham	Oil
	Feering Mill, Essex	Drawing		The afternoon sun, early summer	Oil
1897 Feb	An Old English Gamecock	Oil		Shepherd's hut on the heath	Oil
	Snape	Oil		Bures Water Mill, Suffolk	Oil
	Departing Day	Oil		Bures St. Mary, Suffolk	Oil
	Among the Reeds	Oil		Near neighbours	Oil
	The coming night	Oil	1902	On the Stour, near Bures	Oil
	Snape Bridge – early morning	Oil		Eventide	Oil
	Mares and foals	Oil		A wayside pond	Oil
	Sketches near Hatfield Peverel	Drawing		Early morning	Oil
	Sketch on the Alde – evening	Drawing		The church field	Oil
	Rising mist	Drawing		Old Barn – Theydon Bois, Essex	Drawing
	Mares and foals	Drawing		Near Lyndhurst, Hampshire	Drawing
	Evening – early spring	Oil	1903	Fir Tree Farm, Blaxhall	Oil
1897 Nov	Snape Maltings	Oil		At Farnham, Suffolk	Oil
	A doctor's hack	Oil		Stour – near Bures	Oil
	Little Baddow Mill and Lock, Essex	Oil		On the Alde – late October	Oil
	Tide Mill, Woodbridge	Drawing		In the meadows	Drawing
	Barn at Hatfield Peverel	Drawing		Bures Street, Suffolk	Drawing
	Roadside Church, Layer Breton, Essex	Drawing		Near Hatfield Peverel, Essex	Drawing
	Wenhaston Church	Drawing		Cottage at Lamarsh, Essex	Drawing
	Burnt House Farm	Drawing		Coopersale, near Epping	Drawing
	Cottages at Langford, Essex	Drawing	1905	In the Waveney Valley	Oil
	Snape – from the river wall	Drawing		Early morning	Oil
1898	A plantation at sunset	Oil		The Hall Farm, Dunningworth	Oil
	April	Oil		Meadows at Eleigh	Oil
	On the Alde – nightfall	Oil		Monks Eleigh	Oil
	The railway bridge, Snape	Oil		Oaks at Kirton, Suffolk	Oil
	Langham Bridge	Oil		At Chelsworth, Suffolk	Oil
	Study of a gamecock	Oil	1906	Wortwell Mill on the Waveney	Oil
	The Abbey Farm, Snape – from the river	Oil		Early morning	
	Horses at grass	Drawing		Foalhood	Oil
	A family group	Drawing		Road at Blaxhall	Oil
	Marshes at Wenhaston	Drawing		Blaxhall, Tunstall	Oil
	On the Salting	Drawing		Blaxhall	Oil
1899	On the Heath, Blaxhall	Oil		Springtime	Oil
	Lady Jane Grey	Oil	1907	August	Oil
	Fog	Drawing		In a stack yard	Oil
	Riverside pastures	Drawing		At Stratford St. Mary	Oil
	'What's Up'?	Drawing		The Upper Abbey Farm, Leiston	Oil

	Night – Bures St. Mary	Oil
	The Granary Stairs	Oil
1908	New Comers	Oil
	Near Langham Bridge	Oil
	Playmates	Oil
	Holidays	Oil
	Morning Mist	?
1909	Wanted	Oil
	Towards evening	Oil
	Rising mist	Oil
	What is it?	Oil
	The Hill Farm, Farnham, Suffolk	Drawing
	Charcoal sketch	Drawing
1910	Hackney mares	Oil
	Cottage at Blaxhall	Oil
	After sundown	Oil
	Mouthful of tares	Oil
	At Little Baddow, Essex	Drawing
1911	Horses at grass	Oil
	Snape Street	Oil
	Fresh Pasture	Oil
	Evening – Early Spring (exhibited at RA)	Oil
	A Plantation at Sunset	Oil
	Evening on the Alde	Oil
	Church Cottage, Blaxhall	Oil
	Chelsworth, Suffolk	Oil
	New Comers	Oil

1912	Night – Bures St. Mary – Old house now pulled down	Oil
	In the Gloaming	Oil
	The Granary Stairs	Oil
	Little Baddow Lock and Mill	Oil
	November Evening – Snape Bridge	Oil
	Idle Days	Oil
	Night on the River	Watercolour/ Monochrome
1913	Suffolk Mares and Foals	Oil
	Cronies	Oil
	Mother and Child	Oil
	A Parting Glow	Oil
	In the Gloaming	Oil
	The Footpath	Oil
1914	Botany Farm, Farnham	Oil
	Winter Evening	Oil
	The Colne Valley, Essex	Oil
	By a Suffolk Stream	Oil
	Fordham Heath – Fog Clearing Off	Oil
	Idle Days	Drawing
	An Essex Cottage	Drawing
1915	Sketches	Drawing
	A Homestead	Oil?
	Upper Abbey Farm, Leiston	Oil
	Horses	Oil

APPENDIX 2

Ellen Mary Rope exhibited at the Ipswich Fine Art Club
from 1876 until 1933.

Year	Title	Type
1876	Evangeline	Drawing
	"Kept in"	Drawing
	Night	Drawing
	Fishing	Drawing
	Spring	Drawing
	Seaside	Drawing
1877	One of our pets	Drawing
1878	A study	Painting
	A Gleaner	Painting
	A rustic	Drawing
	On the edge of the Heath	
1879	Broken	Drawing
	Etchings	Drawing
	Winding the Skein	Painting
	An Old Waterloo Soldier in Marylebone Workhouse	Painting
	Study of a child's head	Painting
	The Quarrel and making it up	Painting

Ellen Mary is now seen as an Artist rather than just a club member

Year	Title	Type
1880	A portrait	Painting
	Drawings (pen and ink)	Watercolour
	Peggy in the sulks	Watercolour
	Light and shade	Drawing
	Treasurers	Drawing
	A Gale	Drawing
	Plate	China
	Plate	China
1881	Design for Christmas Card – Youthful Bellringers	Watercolour
	Seaside Sketches	Watercolour
	"Tired Out"	Watercolour
	In the Olden Time	Drawing
	Sketch from Nature	Drawing
	Going Home	Drawing
	Teapot Stand	China
	Plate Peach	China
1882	A Jolly Tar	Painting
	The morning walk	Watercolour
	Design for New Year's card	Watercolour
	Hand-in-hand when our life was May [Gay]	Watercolour
	Study for composition at the Slade School – Joseph's	Monochrome
	Coat brought by his father	Monochrome
	"Tired Out"	Monochrome
1883	A portrait	Painting
	Past and Present in the British Museum	Painting
	Study of a Head	Painting
	Study of a Boy's Head	Painting
	A North Country Maid	Painting
	Book and Beads	Painting
	The Adoration of the Magi (a Slade Composition)	Painting

Year	Title	Type
	Sintram Willing the Storm	Painting
	Giotto discovered by Cimabue	Painting
	In the Green House	Drawing
	A Portrait	Drawing
	Boy's Head	Drawing
	Study of a Child's Head	Drawing
	Sketch from Nature	Drawing
1884	At this stage others in the Rope Clan have started to exhibit E D Rope and Miss E A Rope as well as Ellen Mary and George Thomas	
	Oranges and Lemon	Watercolour
	The Cup found in Benjamins' sack (Slade Composition)	Monochrome
	The Kingdom of the Child	Monochrome
	'Jimmy'	Monochrome
	Study of a Boy	Monochrome
1885	Study of a head	Painting
	'Margie'	Painting
	Young Muscians	Painting
	Sketches Here we come	Monochrome
	Gathering Nuts in May–on the Sands at Iken	Monochrome
	David	Monochrome
	At Rest – By the Wayside	Monochrome
	Pencil Sketch – "Flowers for Teacher"	Monochrome
	Waiting	Drawing
	Daisy Chains	Drawing
	The Young Muscian	Drawing
	Bas-relief, David and Saul	Sculpture
1886	Design fo decoration of a Yacht – Mermaids and Water Babes	Monochrome
	Plaque for Exterior Decoration – Tennis Players (pairs)	Bas Relief
	Cupid Shooting	Bas Relief
	Jog on the footpath Way	Bas Relief
	David and Jonathon	Bas Relief
	Medaliion in Plaster – Margery	Bas Relief
	Cupid preparing to shoot	Bas Relief
	Children on the Apple Bough	Bas Relief
	Sketch at Shere, Surrey	Painting
	Scarlet Runners	Painting
	Little Rachel	Painting
	"Little Tuk", and "Gerda, the Robber Girl" – Designs for Nursery Decoration	Watercclour
	Not Forgotten	Watercolour
	Little Schoolmaster Mark	Monochrome
	In Her Element	Monochrome
1886	Geese	Drawing
	By the Riverside	Drawing
1887	Portrait of an Artist	Painting
	On the Stour – looking for Father	Watercolour
	The Shy Model	Drawing
	Cottage at Straford	Drawing
1888	The New Picture Book	Painting
	A Maid and a Magpie	Painting
	A Young Postman	Painting

Year	Title	Medium
1889	Portrait	Painting
	Children Piping	Plaster
	Demeter and Persephone	Plaster
1890	A Cottage Door	Painting
	Decorative Frieze - Children's Games (Copyright reserved)	Painting
	Lily	
	"Laura"	Pastel
	Cottage at Basildon, Berkshire	Pastel
	"Going a Blackberrying"	Black/White
	Decorated Freize - Children's Games **	Black/White
	Relief in Plaster - Hagar and Ishmael	Plaster
	Relief in Plaster - Ruth and Naomi	Plaster
	One side of cinerary urn, designed for the Cremation Society of England	
	Portrait Medal in Plaster, to be cast in bronze	
1890	"Music" - Decorative Plaque(duplicate Cast in hardened Plaster, Mrs. Laxton Clark's process, can be had at same price)	
	Three Reliefs for decoration of Mantelpiece, children playing, designed and executed for Aldam Heaton Esq.	Watercolour
	Four Reliefs in plaster for decorative Panels (Casts in cement or terra cotta same price, or these Casts can be hardened by Mrs. Laxton Clark's process)	
	Decorative Panel, Children playing in Seaweed	
1891	The Cup found in Benjamin's sack	Watercolour
	Boy on Dolphin	Watercolour
	The Children with Palm Branches (relief in black plaster) to be cast in bronze	Black Plaster
	Mother and Child to be had in bronze	
	"The Sculptor"	
	Zephyrus	
1893	Gleaners	Black/White
	A Water Fairy	
	A Young Violinist	
	Mother and Child - Relief in Bronze	Bronze
1894	Decoration of the East Vestibule, English Section of Women's Building, Chicago Exhibition	Sculptural
	Medallion Portrait of Mrs Henry Fawcett (casts 15s)	Watercolour
	Bas Relief Design for a Panel for Church, executed in bronze or Alabaster	
1895	Mantelpiece Panel – "Children Playing"	Watercolour
	Five Panels – Illustrating Passage from "Troilus and Cressida"	Watercolour
1896	Wood Sprites	Watercolour
	Child Angel – "Least and most child-like of sons of God."	Watercolour
1897	The Guardian Angel (Plaster Relief) or in Bronze (Reproduction of this Cast in Della Robbia ware, glazed or unglazed, can be had from Arnold Rathborne, Esq., Della Robbia Pottery, Birkenhead, at about £5 each	Plaster
	Plaster Relief for Overmantel -	Plaster
	Procession of Children	
	"A merry heart goes all the way"	
	Au Fond de la mer (or in bronze, as exhibited in the Salon at Paris, £10)	
	"Music" - a Panel, in white metal	White metal
	Children with Tortoise (Casts of this can be had at One Guinea each)	
1898	Plaster Panel for Overmantel "Antic, Sport, and blue-eyed pleasures, Frisking light in frolic measures".	Plaster
1899	The Holy Family - Medallion Pottery, in imitation of the old Della Robia Ware.	?
	Spring - Overmantel - Relief	?
	Door-plate, in Bronze Without copyright.	?
	Pair of Door-plates, in Bronze.	?
	Each Design with copyright or casts of Plates. Each Plate, without copyright.	
	A Black Forester	Watercolour
1900	"Here we go round the mulberry"	Watercolour
	Bronze Door Plate	?
	Head	?
1901	Pair of Door Plates	Watercolour
	One of Four Seasons	Watercolour
	One of Four Seasons	Watercolour
	One of Four Seasons	Watercolour
	One of Four Seasons	Watercolour
	Portrait Relief	?
	Mirror Frame Design	Watercolour
	Nursery Panel – Round the Mulberry Tree	?
1902	Panel _ Visit of the Magi	?
	Panel	?
	Child on Squirrel (plaque)	?
	Child on Bird (plaque)	?
1903	Panel for Organ Chamber	Watercolour
	Amphibian	Watercolour
	Nasturtium Fairy	Watercolour
	Sailing towards the Dawn	Watercolour
1904	[No catalogue found at Suffolk Record Office]	
1905	Letter Box Front	?
	Mediating Mischief	Watercolour
	"Caritas"	Watercolour
	Captive Summer and Spring the Deliverer	Watercolour
	Sailing towards the dawn	Watercolour
	Listerning	Watercolour
	Johnny	Watercolour
1906	Winter	Watercolour
	Babes in the Wood	Watercolour
	Amphibian	Watercolour
	Casket in silver and bronze [this piece is attributed to E M Rope & E. Woodward]	
1907	Bellringer No.2	Watercolour
	Bellringer No. 4	Watercolour
	"Et incarnates est"	Watercolour
	"Let the merrie hours go round"	Watercolour
	Bellringer No.1	Watercolour
	Bellringer No.3	Watercolour

1908	Mudlarking	Watercolour
	Bas relief for overmantle – "The valleys stand so thick with corn That they shall laugh and sing."[3] Companion panels, intended for each of a Chancel Screen – "Benedictus qui venit in nominee Domini	?
	Harvester [four]	?
	Winged Mischief	?
1909	"Make a Cheerfull Noise unto the God of Jacob"	?
	Spring [could be brought individually or as set of four]	?
	Tasting	?
	Summer	?
	Hearing	?
	Will o' the Wisp Pleasure	Plaster
	Will o' the Wisp Pleasure	Bronze
	Will o' the Wisp Pleasure	Marble
	Seeing	?
	Autumn	?
	Winter	?
1910	Honeysuckle	Watercolour
	Sweet Pea	Watercolour
	Youthful Modellers	?
	St Cecilia (Memorial Relief)	?
	Fox Glove	Watercolour
	Scarlett Runner	?
	Plaster Relief	Plaster
	A Wooden Stand for Plants, & c., panel of Seasons (woodwork by Arthur Simpson)	Wood & with ceramic
1911	Boys, with Palms(bronze), "Benedictus qui venti"	Bronze
	Flying Fish	?
	"Thou hast revealed it unto babes"	?
	"Thou hast revealed it unto babes"	Marble
	Will – o' the – Wisp – Pleasure	?
	Will – o' the – Wisp – Pleasure	Bronze
	Will – o' the – Wisp – Pleasure	Marble
	Companion panel to Boys, with Palms [see above]	Plaster
	Companion panel to Boys, with Palms [see above]	Bronze
1912	Kneeling Madonna (Statuette)[this piece is attributed to Misses E. M. Rope and D. A. A. Rope] (Exhibited in the R.A.)	Bronze
	Honey Suckle (Flower Fairy)	Watercolour
	Winter	Watercolour
	Daisy (Flower Fairy)	Watercolour
	The Coming of Peace	Plaster
	The Coming of Peace	Bronze
	Life's Morning	?
1913	[No entries from E M Rope this year]	
1914	The Blessed Virgin	?
	Swimming Shield Design	?
	The Angel Gabriel	?

	Nativity, (plaque)	?
1915	The Angel Gabriel	?
	Dance among the Flowers (Portraits)	?
	St Michael	?
	In this year Collection Gift Pictures (Generously presented by the Artists for Sale) The proceeds to be devoted to the Mayoress's Fund for the Wounded	
	Little Modellers	Watercolour
	Winter	Watercolour
	Spring	Watercolour
	Listerning	Watercolour
	The Dark Night	Watercolour
	The Nativity	Watercolour
	Summer	Watercolour
	Mercury	Watercolour
	Pansy	Watercolour
1916	Soldiers All	?
	Pansy	?
	La Paix Qui Vient	?
	Dancing Among Their Flowers	?
1917	[No catalogue found at Suffolk Record Office]	
1918	[No catalogue found at Suffolk Record Office]	
1919	[No entries from E M Rope this year]	
1920	[No entries from E M Rope this year]	
1921	[No entries from E M Rope this year]	
1922	[No catalogue found at Suffolk Record Office]	
1923	[No entries from E M Rope this year]	
1924	[No entries from E M Rope this year]	
1925	[No entries from E M Rope this year]	
1926	A Venture	Plaster
	Four coloured plaques of Flower Fairies	?
	Four plaques of Seasons "Labour Series"	?
	"Thou hast revealed it unto Babies"	Plaster
	Vision of St. Anthony of Padua	Plaster
1927	*Laudanus Te Domini	?
	Annunciation Panel, The Kneeling Virgin	?
	*Adoramus Te Domini	?
	* Companion panels	?
	The Child in the Midst	?
	Memorial to a Harwich Nurse, exhibited at Wembly In chapel arranged by Church Crafts League.	?
1928	Guardian Angel	Bas relief in coloured Plaster
1929	[No entries from E M Rope this year]	
1930	Coloured Panel in Relief	Plaster
	Children bringing Lillies to the Holy Child	?
1931	[No entries from E M Rope this year]	
1932	Lunette in plaster, The Holy Family	Plaster
	Small Plaque, "A Venture"	?
	Bliss	?
	Kneeling Figure of the Holy Virgin [this piece is attributed to Misses E M Rope & D A A Rope]	?
1933	Children of the Week Days	Plaster

REFERENCES

Chapter 1

Bastin, J 1986 The Norfolk Yeomanry in Peace and War, Iceni Press

Chapter 2

Transactions of the Suffolk Naturalists Society' Vol. i. 1929.

Chapter 3

A History of Ipswich Fine Art Club - collection of catalogues Suffolk Record Office - Ipswich Ref. 709.426

'A.F.' The Art Movement: The Work of Miss Ellen M. Rope. *The Magazine of Art.*1900.

Barnes, J., Fagence, S., Heywood, L & Levy, M. 1997. *Ellen Mary Rope, the Poet Sculptor* (exhibition catalogue), H. Blairman & Sons Ltd., London

Beattie, S. 1983. *The New Sculpture.* Yale University Press, London

Chenies Street Chambers Historical Society website: http://www.geocities.com/cheniesuk/brydon.html and http://www.geocities.com/chesiesuk/archive/rope.html

Crawford, E. 2002. *Enterprising Women: the Garretts and their Circle.* Francis Boutle, London.

Darling-Glinski, F. 2003. Ellen Mary Rope, *Sculpture in 20th-century Britain, Volume II.* Henry Moore Institute, Leeds pp.303-4

Graves, A. 1970(a). *Royal Academy exhibitors 1905-1970: a dictionary of artists and their work in the summer exhibitions of the Royal Academy of Arts,* EP Publishing, Wakefield.

Graves, A. 1970(b). *Royal Academy of Arts: a complete dictionary of contributors and their work from its foundation in 1769-1904.* SR Publishers, East Ardsley.

Kendell, B. Miss Ellen Rope, Sculptor. *The Artist,* December 1899, pp.206-212

Maclean F.J. The Art of E.M.Rope. *The Expert,* July 13th, 1907, pp.251-2

McBrinn, J. 2007. *Sophia Rosamond Praeger 1867-1954: Art, Literature Science* (exhibition catalogue). Queen's University, Belfast

Rope, H.E.G. 1931. *Forgotten England and Other Musings,* Heath Cranton, London.

Women's Employments. *Woman at Home,* 1895

Chapter 4

Dunn, G 1977 Popular Singing Traditions in and around Snape and Blaxhall (unpublished Phd thesis Institute of Dialect and Folk Life Studies, University of Leeds)

The Fellowship of Song - Popular Singing Traditions in East Suffolk Dunn, G. 1980 Croom Helm, London